The CHAR GRILLER GRILL & SMOKER COOKBOOK FOR BEGINNERS

OVER 200 DELICIOUS AND EASY SIMPLE RECIPES FOR SMART PEOPLE ON A BUDGET

FREDRICK HILTON

CONTENTS

INTRODUCTION

How the Char Griller Wood Pellet Grill Works

While there are still things that you must do manually as you use a pellet grill, and it is important to pay attention to them, these grills do much of the difficult work for you, like maintaining the desired temperature.

The first thing you must do is fill the hopper with wood pellets. The amount of pellets you will need depends on what kind of cooking you are doing and what temperature will have to be maintained. The manual that comes with the grill should have a guide for this.

Once the grill transfers the wood pellets to the firepot and ignites, you can set the temperature you need with a dial. Lower settings take longer to cook the food, but they also keep the meat moist. This dial will send the information to the auger, the part that transfers pellets.

So long as you put the proper amount of pellets in at the start, the grill will continue cooking for as long as it needs to. Some newer models even have an alert feature that will notify you if the amount of wood pellets gets too low.

The Benefits of Your Char Griller Wood Pellet Grill

1. The Flavor

This is where you have to start this discussion. Yes, there are other benefits you can read about below, but the real benefit of owning a pellet grill is the quality and flavor of the food you can make on them. The reason professional barbecue chefs use wood is because it provides the best flavor. And unlike gas or charcoal, you can vary the flavor with the type of wood pellets you choose, and you can even mix and match to create the perfect flavor for whatever you put on your grill. Our handy find your flavor guide below is great for a quick reference, or you can check out our more detailed guide on selecting the right flavor of pellets.

2. The Ease of Use

Many people get a little intimidated at the thought of using a pellet grill, but those fears are unfounded. Though a pellet grill is different from the standard gas and charcoal grills many people are used to, they're surprisingly user friendly. Char Griller wood pellet grill have controls that you can simply set and forget. Char Griller wood pellet grill offer a number of features that make grilling shockingly easy.

- One button start up – no lighter fluid needed.
- Regardless of the temperature or weather outside, the Grilla and Silverbac keep the temperature within a ten degree range of your set temperature, letting you cook like a pro with zero effort!
- Our pellet grills never have flare ups, so you don't need to worry about your eyebrows.
- You won't oversmoke your food.

With a pellet grill, it's really that easy. You want a perfectly slow smoked brisket? You might be surprised to learn that this doesn't require you to spend 14 hours of your time and attention anymore. With a pellet grill there's no learning curve for making great food. It's literally as easy as filling up the hopper with your preferred flavor of pellets, pushing a button and tossing your meat on the grill. The grill will control the temperature and all you need to do is remove it from the grill when it's done. It can't get any easier than that, can it?

3. The Versatility

Your old gas grill just can't hang with a pellet grill when it comes to the variety of ways you can cook with it. With precise control of cooking temperatures between 180 degrees to 500 degrees you can sear, smoke, roast, and bake with a pellet grill. Why buy a smoker and a grill when you can have both in one well-constructed package? Check out our recipes section to see the incredible range of food you can produce on a pellet grill, everything from brisket, steaks and burgers to shrimp bruschetta and even pecan pie.

Useful Tricks for Using Your Char Griller Wood Pellet Grill

1. USE THE UPPER RACKS OF YOUR Char Griller WOOD PELLET GRILL

Upper racks are great accessories for pellet grills. Not only do they increase the cooking capacity per once grilling session, but upper racks can also decrease the radiant heat releasing from the grease tray.

The meat from the upper racks receives lighter heat, so it is appropriate to cook tender pieces. And the thicker chunk of food can be cooked on the lower rack.

Besides, you can put a water pan under that rack to maintain the ideal temperature for a long brisket cook.

2. USE YOUR Char Griller WOOD PELLET GRILL LIKE YOU USE YOUR OVEN

One of the most straightforward tips to create tastier dishes is to use the pellet grill the same way as using the oven.

Not every food works well with smoke, but how can you know if you haven't tried once, right? Just be brave and creative when mixing the menu, and you can be surprised then.

Any recipe for roasting and baking in your oven can be applied to the smoker. By keeping the same cooking time or alternating cooking period, you can compare how food quality varies between the two devices.

For instance, baking a cake in an oven is too familiar, so why not try grilling in the pellet smoker instead? Making a cake in the oven takes 30 minutes, but you can alternate to 45 minutes or an hour for a grill. The result might come out as not as good as you expect, but, how can you learn if you don't try, right?

3. USE THE REVERSE SEARING

Experienced chefs recommend reverse searing because it can ensure cooked food. Let's go through the process and learn how to do it. Please notice that this method works better on beef slices that are 4 to 5 cm thick.

Firstly, take the meat out from the freezer and wait until it defrosts completely. Then, put the meat on water-absorbing cooking paper to suck water from the meat. Later, warm up the grill at 446 Fahrenheit degree (230 Celsius degree).

The second step is to add salt, sauce, etc. into the food. Wait about 20 minutes for the meat can absorb the mixture better.

Next, put the meat into the pellet smoker for 6 to 8 minutes to reach the medium-rare state (130 Fahrenheit degree/ 54.4 Celsius degree). Then, take out the food and wait for about 5 to 7 minutes.

Finally, half-frying the meat in total 90 seconds with 45 minutes on each side. You should not press the food because juice extraction can decrease the taste of the dish.

4. KEEP TRACK OF THE TEMPERATURE BY USING A THERMOMETER

We are unable to keep track of the inside environment of the smoker just by the sighting. We suggest you use a thermometer to check the heat periodically.

Most people use a clock to set the cooking time so that once it rings, you know whether the dish is ready to serve. However, this is just a presumption based on experience, so there can be risks of overcooking or unripe dishes. So, why don't you choose the safer options instead? A thermometer can solve all these problems.

Besides, there are some grilling experts saying that once you open the grill door, you can't cook anymore. That's true! The heat can escape to the outside environment, and the cooking process will be affected. Hence, it's better to purchase a smoker with an integrated thermometer for a better grilling experience. Also, the integrated thermometer will help you to check the temperature without opening the grill's door.

Significant Tips for Cleaning Your Char Griller Wood Pellet Grill

1. Invest in a Grill Cover.

If a Traeger is stored outside during wet weather, water can get into the Pellet Hopper. When pellets get wet, they expand and can clog the auger. Additionally, a pellet grill cannot cook with wet wood. If you do not have a cover, take extra care to keep the pellet hopper covered and away from any water.

2. Clean your Grease Drain Pan.

Changing the aluminum foil on the grease pan often is a great first step, but to get the most out of your pellet grill you must clean underneath the foil as well. Use a metal spatula to scrape the extra grease and debris from the grease pan and the grease drain tube. Grease is easiest to clean when it is slightly warm. If the grease drain tube becomes plugged or blocked, a grease fire can result. Clean those areas periodically to prevent build-up.

3. Empty your Grease Bucket.

This job is not pretty, but it is pretty easy. Empty your grease into something you can discard, such as a plastic cup. Do not pour grease down the sink drain or into the gutter. Be sure to let the grease cool thoroughly before discarding it. Rinse your bucket with hot, soapy water to remove any remaining grease. To make future clean up easier, line your grease bucket with aluminum foil.

4. Wipe Down your Grill Exterior.

To keep that powder coating looking like new, use warm soapy water to cut through any grease. Do not use oven cleaners, abrasive cleaners, or scouring pads on the outside of your grill.

5. Remove extra ash from the Firepot.

Periodically remove the Porcelain Grill Grate, Grease Drain Pan, and Heat Baffle to clean the ash in and around the Firepot. This step can be fast and easy by using a standard shop vac. Make sure all grill components are cold before vacuuming up the extra ash. We recommend cleaning your grill once for every 5 times you use it. These tips will help keep your grill running beautifully for years to come!

PIZZA

Flat-iron Pizza Quesadillas

Cooking Time: 10 Min

Ingredients:

- 8 Flour Tortillas
- 1 Pack Of Pepperoni And Or Salami
- 2 Cups Of Mozzarella Cheese
- 4 Tbsp Of Butter Or Margarine
- 2 Cups Of Spaghetti Sauce
- 4 Tbsp Of Dried Basil And Or Oregano

Directions:

1. Heat Flat Iron to medium heat. Add butter to flat top and spread across allowing it to melt. Once heated, place 4 tortillas flat on top. Immediately layer cheese, oregano/basil, meat and more cheese on the tortilla. Top with another tortilla. (Optionally, you can make each tortilla its own mini-quesadilla by only layering meat and cheese on one half then folding it in half.) Allow the cheese to fully melt on the inside before using a spatula to flip each over, adding more butter to the flat top, if necessary. Once cheese is melted and tortillas are browned and crisped to your liking, remove from Flat Iron. Serve each quesadilla with spaghetti sauce for dipping. Enjoy!

Gravity 980 Grilled Pizza

Cooking Time: 12 Min

Ingredients:

- 1 Lb. Fresh Pizza Dough
- 1/4 Cup of Extra Virgin Olive Oil
- All Purpose White Flour
- 1 Cup of Fresh Mozzarella Cheese
- Optional Toppings: Pepperoni, Vegetables, Sausage, Bacon, etc.

Directions:

1. Remove the fire shutter from your Gravity 980, load and light the hopper, then preheat to 500-600°F. Add flour to your counter or cutting board before prepping your dough into the desired pizza shape. Add pizza sauce, olive oil and cheese then add your pizza to the pizza stone. Add any toppings that must be cooked then add to the grill. Cook the pizza for 8-12 minutes or until desired brownness. Add any remaining fresh toppings and serve immediately. Enjoy!

Meat Lovers Pizza

Cooking Time: 9 To 12 Min

Ingredients:

- Pre-made Pizza Dough
- Pizza Sauce
- Garlic Powder - 2 tsp
- Shredded Mozzarella - 1 to 1.5 Cups
- 8 to 10 Slices of Pepperoni
- 1-2 Slices of Ham - Chopped
- 1/2 Cup Spicy Sausage - Browned
- 1/2 Cup Ground Beef - Browned
- Parmesan Cheese - Grated
- 1/2 Cup Arugula
- Olive Oil - 1 Tbs
- Salt and Pepper to Taste

Directions:

1. This Meat Lover's pizza packs on the flavor with ham, spicy sausage, ground beef, pepperoni, and two types of cheese. The optional arugula can take it over the top with its peppery bite. Cook

this hot and fast on the AKORN for restaurant quality crust.

2. Allow pizza dough to come up to room temperature (about 8 hours). Tip: Place Pizza Dough in a large plastic bag that seals for the best results.
3. Brown ground beef and spicy sausage. Set aside.
4. Preheat AKORN to 500-600 degrees Fahrenheit. Insert Smokin' Stone. Place Pizza Stone on grates to heat.
5. Shape dough into pizza on a cutting board covered in semolina.
6. Add desired amount of pizza sauce and garlic powder.
7. Add ground beef and sausage to pizza. Add pepperoni and ham. Add mozzarella cheese.
8. Add parmesan cheese to taste.
9. Place pizza on pizza stone. Close lid and cook for 9 minutes or until crust is crisp and cheese melted.
10. Remove from pizza stone and allow to rest for 5 minutes.
11. Toss arugula with olive oil, salt and pepper.
12. Top pizza with arugula if desired.

Grilled Caprese Pizza

Cooking Time: 6 To 8 Min

Ingredients:

- 1 Ball of Pizza Dough, Rolled out Thinly
- 1/2 Cup Pesto
- 1 Small Ball Fresh Mozzarella, Torn to Shreds
- 1/2 Cup Cherry Tomatoes, Halved
- 4-5 Fresh Basil Leaves, Whole or Torn
- 1 Tbsp Fresh Parsley, Chopped
- 1 Tbsp Fresh Parmesan, Shredded or Grated
- 2 Tbsp Olive Oil
- Salt & Pepper to Taste

Directions:

1. Preheat Char-Griller to high heat. Scrape and oil your grates well so the dough does not stick.
2. Spread 1 T of oil to one side of the dough, and place oiled side down on heat first. Immediately turn burners to low and let dough cook for 2-3 minutes that side, until dough bubbles up.
3. Brush remaining oil on uncooked side, and then carefully use spatula to flip dough over. Turn heat off.
4. Spread the dough evenly with pesto, and scatter the torn mozzarella and halved tomatoes over the top. Close the lid, and allow residual heat from the grill to finish cooking the pizza for 5 minutes.
5. Remove pizza from heat and add fresh basil, parsley, and grated parmesan. Serve while warm. Enjoy!

Fire-grilled Pizza

Cooking Time: 10-15 Min

Ingredients:

- 3 C. bread flour
- 2 Tsp. salt
- 3 Tbsp. vegetable oil
- 1 Tsp. sugar
- 1 packet rapid-rising yeast
- 1 C. water
- Corn meal, for dusting
- Tomato sauce
- Garlic powder
- Cheese, if desired
- Toppings of choice

Directions:

1. In a stand mixer fitted with a dough hook, add water and yeast to the bowl and mix well. Then add sugar, salt and vegetable oil and mix.
2. Add bread flour, 1 C. at a time, and mix until a dough forms. Add water as needed to keep dough from sticking to the sides of the bowl. 3. Remove dough and knead for 1 minute by hand, forming it into a ball. Lightly spray a bowl with cooking spray, add dough ball and lightly spray the top. Cover with plastic wrap and allow dough to rise for 1 hour, until doubled in size.
3. Note: Dough is enough to make 2 medium pizzas. Cut dough in half, wrap unused portion and refrigerate or freeze for later use.
4. Pizza
5. Lightly flour counter. Stretch and work dough by hand, kneading until a 12" circle forms. Transfer dough to a wooden pizza peel lightly dusted with corn meal, to prevent sticking. 2. Pre-heat grill to 450°F. Sprinkle pizza dough with garlic powder. Spoon a layer of tomato sauce in the center and spread around to edges of dough. 3. Sprinkle a layer of cheese on top, if desired. Place other toppings on top of cheese layer. 4. Place pizza on pizza stone and allow pizza to cook for 10-15 minutes with lid closed. Rotate pizza after 5 minutes to ensure even cooking. Remove pizza from grill and allow to rest for 4-5 minutes. Slice and enjoy!

Breakfast Pizza

Cooking Time: 10 To 12 Min

Ingredients:

- Pre-made Pizza Dough
- Sun-dried Tomatoes - 1 Cup
- 1 Fresh Mozzarella Ball
- Deli Ham - 4 slices
- 1 Egg
- 1 (8 oz) Jar Tomato Sauce
- Baby Spinach - 2 Cups
- Dried Basil to Taste
- Salt and Pepper to Taste
- Semolina
- Garlic Powder to Taste

Directions:

1. Allow pre-made pizza dough to sit at room temperature covered with a clean dishcloth for at least 6 hours.
2. Preheat grill to medium high heat
3. Add pizza stone to grill and allow to preheat
4. Spread out pre-made pizza dough on a cutting board covered with semolina
5. Cut up ham and spinach.
6. Cut mozzarella into thin slices
7. Add tomato sauce to pizza. (As much as desired.)
8. Season with Garlic Salt and Basil
9. Add mozzarella slices
10. Add ham, spinach, and sun-dried tomatoes.
11. Add extra semolina to pizza stone and carefully slide pizza on grill.
12. Tip: Have a friend help with this step.
13. Allow to cook for 7 minutes with the lid closed.
14. Open grill and crack one egg onto the pizza.
15. Close the lid and allow to cook for 3 to 4 more minutes or until egg white is opaque.
16. Remove from grill and let rest for 5 minutes.
17. Serve and enjoy

Pepperoni Pizza

Cooking Time: 3-5 Min

Ingredients:

- Pizza Dough/Crust
- Pizza Sauce
- Mozzarella Cheese
- Pepperonis
- Other Toppings

Directions:

1. Add a layer of sauce
2. Spread your favorite toppings
3. Add an even layer of cheese
4. Add more toppings if desired
5. Heat grill to 550°F
6. Place pizza on stone
7. Cook for 3-5 minutes
8. Slice and serve!

Grilled Fathead Pizza

Ingredients:

- 10 oz Shredded Mozzarella Cheese
- 1 Egg
- 5 oz Balanced Almond Flour
- 1 tsp Pizza Seasoning
- 1/3 Cup Marinara Sauce
- 1/2 Pound Ground Italian Sausage, Ground
- 15 Pepperoni Slices
- 1 Green Bell Pepper, Chopped
- 1/2 Red Onion, Chopped
- 1 can sliced black olives
- 1 can sliced mushrooms
- 1.5 Cups Shredded Mozzarella Cheese (Topping)

Directions:

1. Preheat grill to a low temp of about 250°.
2. Melt 10 oz mozzarella cheese in microwave in 30 second increments until all melted, add 1 egg & mix. Once egg is mixed add the almond flour, baking powder & pizza seasoning.
3. Knead with hands until well incorporated (for about 3 minutes).
4. Spread dough out on a baking sheet with parchment paper.
5. Put on grill for about 5-6 minutes until crust is turning golden.
6. Then take crust off the grill, flip over & put back on parchment paper.
7. Add toppings & then put back in the grill for about 10 minutes or until desired doneness.

Pesto Burrata Grilled Pizza

Cooking Time: 3 Min

Ingredients:

- 1 Pizza Dough Ball (Store bought Dough or Homemade Dough)
- 1 Cup pesto
- 1 Cup Fresh Greens (Arugula or Spinach)
- 2 Burrata Balls
- 1/2 Cup Fresh Basil Leaves
- 4 T Olive Oil
- Salt And Pepper To Taste

Directions:

1. Fill chimney with charcoal. Place over side burner and turn flame to high, allowing charcoal to catch fire. If you do not have the side burner on your Texas Trio, you can light paper under the chimney so that it catches. We are cooking on the Akorn Jr today, so prep the base for charcoal, scrape the grates to make sure they're clean, and grab your stone or cast iron for the pizza.
2. Once coals have heated through, about 20 minutes, add them to the base of the Akorn Jr

and place grates over the coals, add cast iron, and close lid to allow grill to heat up.

3. Let's prep the pizza. Cut dough ball into four equal pieces and roll each piece out to a thin circle.

4. I like to plate up all my toppings and take them out to the grill so I can make the pizzas quickly. When it's time- add a drizzle of the olive oil to the stone or cast iron and lay the dough out. Flip after about 60 seconds, once the sides start to golden and you see some bubbles forming. On the now cooked side that is up- spread ¼ cup of the pesto, add half a ball of burrata and close the lid for an additional 1-2 minutes, until the pie is cooked through. Remove from heat and top with arugula, fresh basil leaves, a drizzle of olive oil, and salt and pepper. Repeat three more times until all the pies are done. Serve hot, and enjoy!

Flat Iron Cheesy Pizza Bagels

Cooking Time: 15 Min

Ingredients:

- 3 Bagels Cut in Halves (Whatever type you prefer)
- 1 Can of Pizza Sauce
- 1 Cup of Pepperoni or Salami (Sliced)
- 2 Cups of Mozzarella Cheese
- 2 Tbsp of Butter

Directions:

1. Melt 1 Tbsp of butter on Flat Iron over Medium Heat.
2. Place bagels face down in butter and allow 2-3 minutes for them to lightly toast. Remove from heat.
3. On a separate section of the griddle, warm pepperoni/salami over medium heat for 3-4 minutes then set aside
4. On a tray or large plate, assemble bagel pizzas by spreading each with sauce, then adding desired amount of pepperoni/salami and cheese on top.
5. Place each bagel pizza back on the griddle on another Tbsp of melted butter over on medium-low heat until cheese has thoroughly melted and the bottom is toasted. (It might help to cover each bagel pizza with a basting/grill cover)
6. Serve hot.

POULTRY

Creole Smokin' Fried Wings

Cooking Time: 1 Hrs

Ingredients:

- 16-20 chicken wings
- 1/2 Tbsp Creole seasoning
- 1/2 Tbsp adobo seasoning
- 1 Tbsp sazón seasoning
- 12 oz. buffalo sauce
- Olive Oil
- All-vegetable shortening

Directions:

1. Coat wings in even layer with olive oil in a large bowl or plastic bag
2. Season with Creole, Adobo & Sazón
3. Place wings in fridge for at least on hour to allow the seasoning to absorb into the wings.
4. Heat grill to 340°F
5. Place wings in grill and smoke with apple wood chunks or your favorite
6. Smoke for 30 mins or until the wings reach internal temp of 140°F
7. Remove wing and place in pan. Set aside pan.
8. Add charcoal to grill and get extremely hot for frying the wings in the cast iron skillet
9. Add all-vegetable shortening to cast iron skillet and then place on grill allowing to heat up
10. Place small batch of wings into skillet and fry for 2-3 minutes or until crispy
11. Remove from skillet and place on baking rack in pan
12. Warm your favorite buffalo sauce
13. Toss wings in warmed buffalo sauce
14. Serve with ranch or blue cheese, carrots, and celery.

Creole Latin Spiced Rotisserie Chicken

Ingredients:

- Whole Chicken (Any Size)
- Olive Oil
- Creole Seasoning To Taste
- Sazon To Taste
- Adobo To Taste
- Fresh Parsley Flakes or Fresh Cilantro Flakes
- Kitchen Twine
- 1 Onion (Sliced)
- Char-Griller Grills Super Pro & Rotisserie Kit

Directions:

1. Rinse and pat dry chicken. Trim access fat and skin. Apply coating of olive oil to all sides of the chicken. Add Sazon, Creole and adobo seasonings. Add twine and knot the legs and also the wings over the breast. Add chicken to rotisserie rod and lock in using the rotisserie forks. Then Sprinkle fresh parsley or cilantro flakes on to the chicken. Slice onion and place on to a hook. Heat grill with lump charcoal: When coking over an open fire I don't cook at specific temperature. I begin with an equivalent of a 1/2 chimney full of lump charcoal and monitor the fire by feel. I place the charcoal in the middle of the grill in the back. As the charcoal burns I add pieces as the cook goes along. Place rotisserie chicken in the grill along with the onions. Roast chicken until internal 165°. Remove chicken and onions from the grill. Allow to rest for 15 minutes. Slice and enjoy!

Easy Chicken And Cheese Quesadillas

Cooking Time: 10 Min

Ingredients:

- Pack Of Soft Tortillas
- 2 Lbs Chicken Tenderloin
- Your Choice of Cheese
- Your Choice Of Other Toppings

Directions:

1. Bring your griddle to high / medium-high heat, throw down some oil and cook up your chicken. Once they are cooked and chopped up, move them off to the side.
2. Throw down a little more oil because the griddle may be pretty dry by now, then a couple of tortillas to brown and soften up.
3. After flipping the tortillas once, add your toppings. Start with cheese all over the tortillas, then add your other toppings only on one half of the tortilla.
4. Fold the tortilla in half to create your quesadilla. Press firmly to activate the 'cheese glue'.
5. Flip once more to ensure everything is melty goodness inside.
6. Cut with a pizza cutter and serve with your choice of dips!

Grilled Chicken And Broccoli Stir-fry

Cooking Time: 10 Min

Ingredients:

- 1 lb. chicken breast
- 8 oz. bottle Italian dressing
- 1 Tbsp. extra-virgin olive oil
- 1 head broccoli, stemmed and cut into florets
- ½ red pepper, sliced
- ½ green pepper, sliced
- ½ yellow pepper, sliced
- ½ red onion, sliced
- 1 Tbsp. dried basil
- 1 Tbsp. dried oregano
- 1 Tbsp. garlic powder
- Olive oil, for brushing
- Salt and pepper, to taste

Directions:

1. Rinse chicken and pat dry with paper towel. Pour Italian dressing into a large resealable plastic bag, add chicken and gently shake to evenly coat. Marinate for 2–3 hours in the refrigerator, or best overnight.
2. Rinse produce and pat dry with paper towel. Pre-heat grill to 400°F and brush a grill wok with olive oil.
3. Remove chicken from marinade, cut into 1" thick strips and place in grill wok. Discard dressing.
4. Sear the chicken strips evenly on all sides, until golden brown, for about 3 minutes.
5. Add the broccoli, red pepper, green pepper, yellow pepper, and red onion to the wok and cook for about 5 minutes, stirring occasionally.
6. Mix together basil, oregano and garlic powder in a small bowl to make seasoning and add salt and pepper, to taste. Sprinkle over chicken and vegetables and stir to combine.
7. Serve over cooked rice and garnish with fresh basil and chopped cashews or peanuts, if desired.

Creole Latin Spatchcock Turkey

Cooking Time: 1-2 Hrs

Ingredients:

- Whole turkey
- Kitchen Scissors & Pairing Knife
- Char-Griller Marinade Injector
- Creole Seasoning: Generous Coating
- Sazón Seasoning: Generous Coating
- Adobo Seasoning
- Garlic Powder
- Onion Powder
- Creole Butter Injectable Marinade (17 Oz)
- Fresh or Dry Cilantro
- Olive Oil
- Turkey Oven Bags
- Bucket Or Cooler
- Char-Griller Grill

Directions:

1. Chop up fresh cilantro and set aside.

2. Remove turkey from bag & remove everything inside the cavity area along with the plastic tie holding the legs. 3.Using kitchen scissors & pairing knife remove the backbone to Spatchcock the turkey. Also trim and remove any access fat & skin.

3. Flip Turkey breast side up & push down on the breast using both hands to help flatten the turkey.

4. Inject turkey with Creole Butter. Use any extra Creole & rub on breast under skin.

5. Generously add olive to the both sides of the turkey.Tip: continue to trim access fat & skin as you go along.

6. Generously season the turkey with Adobo, Sazón, Creole, onion powder & garlic powder. Then sprinkle cilantro 8. Place turkey in turkey/oven bag & place in bucket or cooler. Place in refrigerator & allow the turkey to rest for 12-24 hours. Cooking Directions 1. Remove turkey from bucket/cooler & allow to rest at room temperature for 1-2 hours. 2. Preheat your Char-griller Smoker to 240°. 3. Place turkey in smoker and smoke until the turkey reaches 165° internal temperature. Product tip: use the Char-griller remote thermometer or folding prob thermometer. 4. Check on turkey about every hour & baste turkey with butter & spritz with apple juice. Tip: rotate turkey in different directions to allow even cooking. 5. After turkey reaches 165° internal temperature allow the turkey to rest for a minimum of 25 minutes. Sprinkle additional cilantro. 7. Slice, serve & enjoy.

Chicken Cordon Bleu

Cooking Time: 20 Min

Ingredients:

- 2-3 Chicken breasts
- 6 strips of bacon
- 2 slices deli ham
- 4 slices of cheese
- Jalapeños, seeded and sliced, optional
- Garlic powder
- Salt and pepper, to taste

Directions:

1. Rinse chicken breasts and pat dry with paper towel. Place inside a resealable plastic bag and flatten using a mallet, until about a ½" thick. 2. Remove chicken from bag and layer a slice of ham and 2 slices of cheese on each. Place jalapeño slices on each, if desired. 3. Tightly roll chicken breast, keeping ham and cheese inside. Wrap each breast with 3 slices of bacon and lightly season with garlic powder, salt and pepper on

both sides, to taste. Refrigerate for 10-20 minutes.
4. Pre-heat grill to 400°F and place chicken directly on grates, for about 20 minutes, flipping halfway through for good sear marks. Chicken is done when internal temperature reaches 165°F.
2. Slice, serve and enjoy!

Grilled Nachos

Cooking Time: 25-30 Min

Ingredients:

- 3 boneless skinless chicken breasts
- 6 mini sweet peppers
- 1 bag of tortilla chips
- 1 8oz. bag of shredded fiesta cheese
- 1 jar of your favorite salsa
- Original All-Purpose BBQ rub, or your favorite rub

Directions:

1. Heat grill to 325°F.
2. While grill is heating, rub the chicken breasts liberally with your favorite rub or use Original All-Purpose BBQ rub, to taste.
3. Place chicken breasts on the grill and cook for 6 minutes per side until internal temperature reaches 165°F, flipping halfway through for good sear marks.
4. Remove chicken and chop into chunks. Chop up sweet peppers.
5. In a grill safe pan, layer chips, chicken, peppers and cheese for three layers.
6. Place pan on the grill and grill for 12-15 minutes.
7. Once cheese is melted, remove from the grill and top with your favorite salsa.
8. Enjoy!

Smoked Turkey Legs

Cooking Time: 3.5 Hrs

Ingredients:

- 1 Gallon of Water
- 1 cup of Kosher Salt
- 2 Tbsp of Garlic (Minced)
- 2 Tbsp of Ground Black Pepper
- 4 Tbsp of Garlic Powder
- 4 Tbsp of Onion Powder
- 1/3 Cup of Brown Sugar
- 2 Tbsp of Dried Basil
- 2 Tbsp of Dried Sage
- 2 Tbsp of Dried Thyme
- 1 Tsp of Paprika
- 1 Tsp of Cayenne Pepper
- 2-3 Bay Leaves

Directions:

1. Combine all the brine recipes in a large pot and bring to a boil. Let it cool. As it boils, rinse the turkey legs. Once the brine cools, submerge the turkey legs in it. Cover and refrigerate it overnight. Heat your smoker to 225-250°F. Remove the turkey legs from the refrigerator and pat dry with paper towels, allowing them to sit for 15-20 minutes. Transfer the turkey legs to the smoker and cook for 3-4 hours until the legs have a dark exterior and the juices run clear.
2. Allow them to rest for 10-15 minutes before serving as is, with barbecue sauce and with any desired sides

Turkey-mushroom Burger

Cooking Time: 20 Min

Ingredients:

- 1¼ lb. ground turkey
- 1 large Portobello mushroom cap
- 1 Tbsp. shallot, coarsely chopped
- 3 Tbsp. fresh parsley
- 2 Tbsp. olive oil
- 1 Tsp. Worcestershire sauce
- 8 thin slices white cheddar cheese
- 4 Hamburger buns
- Salt and pepper, to taste
- Avocado slices, for topping
- Condiments of choice

Directions:

1. Pre-heat grill to 375°F. Clean the mushroom cap, remove the gills and cut into 1" pieces. Transfer to a food processor and add the shallot and parsley; pulse until chopped. 2. Combine mushroom mixture, turkey, olive oil, Worcestershire sauce, 1 Tsp. salt, and pepper to taste in a large bowl. Mix by hand until just blended. Divide into 4 balls, and form 1" thick patties. Put on a large plate, cover and refrigerate until firm, about 30 minutes. 3. Grill the patties for 4- 5 minutes on each side, with a quarter turn halfway through for good sear marks. Top each with 2 slices of cheese during the last 3 minutes of cooking and allow cheese to melt. Toast hamburger buns on the grill until lightly browned. Allow burgers to rest for 5 minutes before serving.
2. Serve the turkey burgers on hamburger buns and top with avocado slices and condiments of choice.

Gravity 980 Smoked Chicken Wings

Cooking Time: 2.5 Hrs

Ingredients:

- 2 lb. of fresh, thawed Chicken Wings
- 2 Tbsp of Extra Virgin Olive Oil
- 1/4 Cup of Char-Griller Chicken Rub
- 1 Tsp of Cumin
- 1 Tsp of Cayenne Powder

Directions:

1. If you prefer to rinse your chicken wings, do so in cold water. Pat them completely dry with paper towels. In a resealable bag, combine olive oil, and all seasonings, then add chicken and seal bag. Thoroughly mix chicken and oil mixture within bag until all pieces are coated. Place in the refrigerator and allow to sit for 1 hour through overnight. Remove the fire shutter from the Gravity 980, load and light the hopper then set to 225-250°F. Place chicken wings in the grill in a single layer and smoke for 2 to 2 ½ hours or until the internal temperature reaches 165°F. Allow wings to rest for 10-20 minutes then serve. Enjoy!

Chicken Fajitas

Cooking Time: 20 Min

Ingredients:

- 1 lb. chicken breasts, filleted in half
- 1 ½ Tsp. seasoned salt
- 1 ½ Tsp. dried oregano
- 1 ½ Tsp. ground cumin
- 1 Tsp. garlic powder
- ½ Tsp. chili powder
- ½ Tsp. paprika
- 2 Tbsp. lemon juice
- 2 Tbsp. vegetable oil

- 1 onion, thinly sliced
- 1-2 bell peppers, cored, stemmed and thinly sliced
- Pico de Gallo, for serving
- Shredded cheese, for serving
- Tortillas

Directions:

1. Rinse chicken and pat dry with paper towel. Pour dry ingredients, lemon juice and vegetable oil into a large resealable plastic bag, add chicken and gently shake to evenly coat. Marinate for 2–3 hours in the refrigerator, or best overnight. 2. Pre-heat grill to 400°F. Place chicken directly on the grill and sear for 5-7 minutes on each side, flipping halfway through for good sear marks. Chicken is done when internal temperature reaches 165°F. Remove chicken from grill and wrap in foil to keep warm. 3. While chicken is searing, place 1-2 Tbsp. of oil on a heated cast iron fajita pan. Using a heat resistant grill glove, carefully pick up the pan and spread the oil around evenly. Place the onions and peppers on the pan and sauté for 5-7 minutes until softened. 4. Toast tortillas on warming rack for 5 minutes. Unwrap chicken from foil and slice into 1" thick strips.
2. To serve, spoon a layer of Pico de Gallo and cheese on tortilla. Top with a layer of peppers and onions and add chicken. Enjoy!

Chili Mesquite Lime Shredded Chicken Street Tacos

Cooking Time: 45 Min

Ingredients:

- 6 Tbsp Mesquite Lime Sea Salt
- 2 Tbsp Chili Powder
- 1 Lime (Squeezed)
- 4 Chicken Breasts (Skinless)
- Chili Lime Sauce
- 1 Package Provolone Cheese Slices

Directions:

1. Mix sea salt, powder and lime together Trim any excess fat off chicken breasts Season chicken with sauce and let sit for 10-15 mins Get your grill up to temp at about 400° - 450° Place chicken on grill until IT of 165° Pull chicken and place in the Instant Pot for 30 mins (add 1/2 cup water) Shred chicken and place on shells, top with pico de gallo and Sriracha Warm up a pan and throw cheese slice in pan When cheese begins to bubble flip over until brown

Picnic "fried" Chicken

Cooking Time: 35 Min

Ingredients:

- 6 bone-in chicken thighs
- 3 Tbsp. Chicken BBQ rub
- 2 C. dried bread crumbs
- 2 eggs, beaten
- ½ C. buttermilk

Directions:

1. Rinse chicken thighs and pat dry with paper towel.
2. Prepare breading by mixing Chicken BBQ rub with bread crumbs in gallon sized storage bag.
3. Whisk eggs with buttermilk in large bowl until smooth. Dip chicken thighs in egg/buttermilk mixture and evenly coat all sides.
4. Place chicken thighs in bag with breading mixture, seal bag and shake gently to even coat thighs on all sides.
5. Place breaded chicken thighs on a cast iron griddle in the middle of the grill at 375°F for 35 minutes. Chicken thighs are done when internal temperature reaches 165°F.

Honey Chipotle Chicken Wings

Cooking Time: 15 Min

Ingredients:

- 2 lbs. chicken wings
- 2 oz. apple cider vinegar
- 4 oz. honey
- 2 Tbsp. chipotle pepper
- 2 oz. mustard
- 1-2 Tsp. red pepper flakes
- 4 oz. olive oil
- Salt and pepper to taste

Directions:

1. Mix mustard, red pepper flakes, honey, chipotle peppers, and apple cider vinegar to make chipotle sauce
2. Slowly infuse olive oil slowly while stirring
3. Season with salt and pepper and stir
4. Using only half the sauce, toss the chicken wings in the sauce and set aside the remaining half
5. Place wings on the grill at 350°F, cook for 7-8 minutes
6. Flip wings, and cook another 7-8 minutes
7. Remove wings and toss in the remaining sauce

Cherry Chipotle Buffalo Wings

Cooking Time: 1 Hrs

Ingredients:

- 4 lbs. chicken wings
- 14 oz. bottle cherry Chipotle BBQ sauce
- 3 Tsp. dried minced onion
- 2 Tsp. Chipotle chili powder
- 1 ½ Tsp. garlic powder
- 1 ½ Tsp. chili powder
- ½ Tsp. smoked paprika
- 2 C. sour cream
- 1 C. blue cheese salad dressing
- 1 C. blue cheese, crumbled
- 1 C. green onions, thinly sliced
- Salt and pepper, to taste

Directions:

1. Combine 1 Tsp rub, sour cream, salad dressing, crumbled blue cheese and green onions together in a medium bowl and mix well. 2. Refrigerate at least 2 hours to blend flavors.

2. Buffalo wings

3. Rinse chicken wings and dry with paper towel.

2. Combine dried minced onion, Chipotle chili powder, garlic powder, chili powder, smoked paprika and salt and pepper, to taste, into a small bowl and mix well. Reserve 1 Tsp. to mix with dipping sauce. Season chicken wings generously with rub. Place wings on the grill, equally spaced in rows, to smoke for 30 minutes when grill temperature reaches 250°F. 4. After letting wings smoke, increase grill temperature to 350°F and cook wings until internal temperature reaches 165°F. 5. Brush on sauce during the last 15 minutes, flipping once and coating evenly every 5 minutes.

Turkey Tips

Cooking Time: 3½ Hrs

Ingredients:

- 7-8 lb. turkey breast, cubed
- 1 medium onion, thinly sliced
- Chicken BBQ rub
- BBQ sauce
- 1-2 Tbsp. butter
- Salt and pepper, to taste

Directions:

1. Place turkey in a large roasting pan in an even layer, add BBQ sauce and turn to evenly coat. Allow to marinate for an hour.
2. Pre-heat grill to 230°F. Place pan with turkey on the grill and smoke for 30 minutes per pound or until internal temperature reaches 165°F.
3. While turkey is smoking, place a cast iron skillet on the grill and heat until very hot.
4. Remove turkey from roasting pan and add to skillet with onions, butter and more BBQ sauce. Allow to smoke for an additional 25 minutes, stirring occasionally.

Flat Iron East Meets West Chicken Fajitas

Cooking Time: Varies Min

Ingredients:

- 6 Chicken Breasts, Cut into Fajita Slices
- 4 Green Peppers, Cut into Slices
- 4 Yellow Peppers, Cut into Slices
- 2 Large Onions, Sliced
- 2 Packs Tortillas
- 2 Eggs
- 2 Tbsp Soy Sauce
- 1 Tbsp Brown Sugar
- 1 tsp Fresh Ginger, Minced
- 2 Cups Cooked Rice
- Sesame Oil
- Sesame Seeds
- 4 Scallions, Sliced
- Char-Griller Chicken Rub
- Salt and Pepper to Taste

Directions:

1. Taking traditional fajita flavors and adding and extra twist to it, you can cook this whole meal on the Flat Iron at one time! Fried rice, marinated chicken, veggies and toasted tortillas all come together to make this great dish.
2. Pre-heat griddle on Medium High
3. Slice chicken breasts into fajita slices
4. Slice peppers, onions, and scallions
5. Mix together soy sauce, brown sugar and ginger. Pour over chicken in bowl and toss to coat
6. Create 4 cooking zones, high, medium high, medium and low
7. Spread sesame oil on griddle
8. Place chicken on high cooking zone and peppers and onions on medium high cooking zone
9. Season peppers and onions with salt and pepper.
10. Place rice on medium cooking zone.
11. Make a circle of oil, crack two eggs into it. Add Char-Griller Chicken Rub to taste and scallions. Scramble eggs.
12. Add eggs to rice and mix well to incorporate. Add more soy sauce to rice if desired.
13. Check on chicken and vegetables. Flip if needed.
14. Place tortillas on low cooking zone to toast.
15. After chicken reaches 165, remove from grill and build fajitas with chicken, peppers, onions, and rice.
16. Garnish with extra scallions and sesame seeds.

Spicy Honey Glazed Wings

Cooking Time: 25 Min

Ingredients:

- 3 Lbs Chicken Wings
- A.Vogel Spicy Herbed Sea Salt
- Mikes Hot honey

Directions:

1. Preheat grill to 350F. Season wings with spicy herbed sea salt. Grill wings direct to an internal temperature of 190F. Remove from heat and glaze with Mikes hot honey. Serve and enjoy!

Creole Hush Puppy Fried Chicken Legs & Thighs

Ingredients:

- 4 Chicken Legs & 4 Thighs
- 2 Cups of Milk
- Garlic Parsley Butter
- CharGriller Creole Seasoning
- Caribeque Lemon Garlic Seasoning
- 2 Tbs of Sazon
- Garlic Powder To Taste
- Black Pepper To Taste
- Crispy Creole Tony Chachere's Hush Puppy 9.5 Oz
- 1 Cup of All Purpose Flour
- 1/2 Cup of Panko Bread Crumbs
- Cayenne Pepper To Taste
- Lard For Frying
- Char-Griller Grills Hybrid Gas and Charcoal Grill With a Side Burner

Directions:

1. Garlic Parsley Buttermilk Prepping
2. In a large bowl add 2 cups Milk Add melted Garlic Parsley Butter: 4 oz. to the milk. -Full Garlic Parsley Recipe links: Written Recipe & Video Recipe Add Char-Griller Grills Lemon Pepper: to taste Add Caribeque Lemon Garlic: to taste Add Black Pepper to Taste Add Garlic powder to Taste Add Creole Seasoning to Taste Mix ingredients thoroughly. Rinse and clean the chicken legs and thighs with cold water and pat dry with a paper towel. Trim any fat or cartilage from the chicken. Place the chicken in the Garlic Parsley Butter Mixture and mix thoroughly. Place in the fridge for 6-24 hours.
3. Batter/Breading Prep
4. In a large pan add the hush puppy mix: 9.5 oz., All Purpose Flour: one cup and Panko Bread Crumbs: ½ cup Add Cayenne Pepper: to taste Add Creole Seasoning: to taste Add Sazon: 2 tbs Add Black Pepper: to taste Mix all the ingredients thoroughly. Remove the chicken from the fridge and bowl. Then place the chicken legs and thighs in the batter/breading. Tip: apply pressure onto the chicken so the batter/breading can be thickly applied to the chicken. Set aside while the cast iron skillet heats up.
5. Cooking Directions
6. Fire up your Char-Griller Grills Hybrid Gas and Charcoal Grill side burner using a large cast iron skillet with lard. Preheat the Cast Iron Skillet with the oil to 335°. Place the chicken into the cast iron skillet for 15 minutes or until internal temperature 175°. Tip: place the chicken thighs skin side down when placing into the cast iron skillet. Remove the chicken from the cast iron skillet and allow it to drain/cool for 7 minutes. Serve and Enjoy

Garlic Lover's Chicken

Cooking Time: 10 Min

Ingredients:

- 7 lb. whole chicken
- 16 oz. bottle Italian dressing
- 4-5 handfuls peeled garlic cloves, to taste
- 2 Tbsp. butter, melted
- 1 Tsp. olive oil
- 2 Tsp. dried thyme leaves
- 1 Tsp. seasoned salt
- 2 Tsp. white pepper

- 2 Tbsp. flour
- 1 C. low fat milk
- 2 C. dry white wine
- Garlic dry rub or Chicken BBQ rub, to taste

Directions:

1. Rinse chicken, dry with paper towel and cut in half. Marinate chicken halves in Italian dressing for four hours, or overnight. Season generously with garlic dry rub or use Chicken BBQ rub.
2. Roast chicken on the grill at 400°F for 45 minutes. Chicken is done when internal temperature reaches 170°F. Remove chicken from the grill and let rest 5-10 minutes.
3. Garlic sauce
4. Sauté garlic cloves in a medium sauce pan with butter and olive oil until lightly browned. Stir frequently and cook until garlic is soft, 5-7 minutes.
5. Whisk together flour, milk, white wine, thyme and white pepper in a small bowl. Add to garlic, stir to combine and simmer for 10 minutes.
6. To serve, pour garlic sauce over baked chicken halves and enjoy!

Izzy's Cowboy Grillers

Cooking Time: 20 Min

Ingredients:

- 8 Chicken Breasts
- 1 Block Pepper Jack Cheese
- 1 Lb Bacon
- Jalapeño Slices
- All Purpose Seasoning (Pappys Blue Label Is What I Used)

Directions:

1. Slice a pocket in the middle of each chicken breast and place jalapeño slices and a slice of pepper jack cheese inside. Preheat grill to 325F. Wrap each prepared chicken breast in 2 pieces of bacon. Season using your favorite all purpose rub. Grill direct at 325F to an internal temp of 165F. Remove, serve and enjoy!

Barbecued Turkey

Cooking Time: 4 Hrs

Ingredients:

- 13 lb. turkey, cut into pieces
- 1/2 C. Chicken BBQ rub
- BBQ sauce for brushing

Directions:

1. Season both sides of turkey pieces generously with Chicken BBQ rub, or your favorite rub.
2. Smoke turkey pieces on the grill on direct heat at 225°F for 3 hours and then raise the temperature to 350°F for another hour to finish it off.
3. Brush one side of turkey pieces with BBQ sauce at the 30-minute mark.
4. Flip and brush the other side after 15 minutes. Remove turkey pieces when internal temperature reaches 165°F.
5. Note: The turkey's internal temperature will continue to increase by 5-10 degrees after you pull it off the grill.

Beer Can Roasted Turkey Breast

Cooking Time: 4-5 Hrs

Ingredients:

- Turkey Breast
- Favorite Rub/Seasonings: Blues Hog Sweet & Savory and a 50/50 blend of Coarse Salt & Coarse Pepper.
- Olive Oil

- Char-Griller Grills Beer Can Chicken Rack with Beer Can
- Char-Griller Grills Ceramic Akorn Kamado Charcoal Grill, Smokin' Stone & Drip Pan
- Fuel: Fogo Eucalyptus Lump Charcoal
- Char-Griller Grills Folding Probe

Directions:

1. -pound turkey breast with bones: Trim all loose fat and skin. Place the turkey breast on the Beer Can Chicken Rack Apply olive oil to all the sides of the turkey. Season all sides of the meat with your favorite Char-Griller Rub/Seasonings. Preheat grill/smoker to 250°. Once the grill/smoker is preheated, add the Smokin' Stone & Char-Griller Drip Pan filled with water to the grill/smoker. Remember to use your Char-Griller Grills Probe to take the guess work out your cooking. Place turkey in grill/smoker and smoke until internal temperature 165° is met, roughly takes 4-5 Hours
2. Tip: while smoking, if a spot on the meat/skin gets too much char, place a small piece of foil
3. Over the spot to help prevent that spot from burning/drying out. Rotate in the smoker/grill every 45 minutes and rotate the turkey for even cooking. Remove from the smoker/grill and allow to rest for 15-30 minutes. Slice and enjoy.

Grilled Chicken And Vegetable Kebabs

Cooking Time: 15 Min

Ingredients:

- 2 lbs. boneless, skinless chicken thighs
- 1 C. whole yogurt
- 2 Tbsp. unsalted butter, melted
- 1 Tbsp. salt
- ½ Tsp. ground coriander
- ¼ Tsp. ground turmeric
- Pinch red pepper flakes, optional
- 1 garlic clove, finely grated
- 3 bell peppers, stemmed and cored
- 1 red onion, cut into wedges
- 2 Tbsp. olive oil
- Flatbread, for serving
- Fresh mint and parsley leaves, chopped, for garnish
- Bamboo skewers

Directions:

1. Rinse chicken, pat dry with paper towel and cut into 2" thick pieces. Whisk together yogurt, butter, salt, coriander, turmeric, red pepper flakes and grated garlic in a medium bowl until smooth.
2. Add chicken and toss to evenly coat. Cover bowl with plastic wrap and let marinate at room temperature for 1 hour.
3. Rinse produce. Slice peppers into 2" thick pieces. Toss peppers and onion wedges in a medium bowl with the olive oil, and season with salt, to taste.
4. Soak bamboo skewers in water for 30 minutes. Divide chicken and vegetables evenly between the skewers, alternating between the two.
5. Pre-heat grill to 400°F. Grill kebabs, turning as needed, until the chicken has cooked through, about 15-20 minutes. Chicken is done when internal temperature reaches 165°F.
6. Let rest for 3-5 minutes, then garnish with chopped mint and parsley leaves, and serve with flatbread.
7. Enjoy!

Smoked Spatchcock Turkey

Cooking Time: 3-4 Hrs

Ingredients:

- 12-20 lb. turkey
- 3/4 C. olive oil
- 3 Tbsp. minced garlic
- 2 Tbsp. fresh rosemary, chopped
- 1 Tbsp. fresh basil, chopped
- 1 Tbsp. Italian seasoning
- 1 Tsp. ground black pepper

Directions:

1. In a small bowl, mix the olive oil, garlic, rosemary, basil, Italian seasoning, black pepper and salt. Set aside. 2. Rinse the turkey inside and out; pat dry. Loosen the skin from the breast. Work it loose to the end of the drumstick being careful not to tear the skin.

2. Tip: This is easily done by slowly working your fingers between the breast and the skin.

3. Using your hand, spread a generous amount of the rosemary mixture under the breast skin and down the thigh and leg. Rub the remainder of the rosemary mixture over the outside of the breast and all over the turkey. 4. Place turkey in your smoker, and smoke at 250°F for 3 to 4 hours, or until the turkey internal temperature reaches a minimum of 165°F.

Grilled Duck Breast

Cooking Time: 20 Min

Ingredients:

- 8 skinned, boned duck breast halves
- ½ Tsp. hot sauce
- 2 Tbsp. minced garlic
- ¼ C. Worcestershire sauce
- ¼ Tsp. black pepper

Directions:

1. Whisk together Worcestershire sauce, olive oil, hot sauce, garlic, and pepper in a large bowl.
2. Rinse duck breasts and pat dry with paper towel. Score the skin of the duck with a sharp knife in a ¼" diamond pattern to render out the fat for crispy skin.
3. Add the duck breasts to bowl and toss well to coat. Cover with plastic wrap and marinate in the refrigerator for 30 minutes or best overnight.
4. Pre-heat grill to 375°F and put an aluminum pan under the grates to catch drippings. Grill the duck, skin side down, for 4-5 minutes per side.
5. Duck is done when internal temperature reaches 135°F for medium-rare. Remove from the grill and allow to rest 5-10 minutes before slicing and serving.

2-burner Flat Iron Seasoned Chicken Breasts

Cooking Time: 20 Min

Ingredients:

- 4 Boneless Chicken Breasts
- 1/4 Cup of Extra Virgin Olive Oil
- 1 Lemon
- 1 Tbsp of Garlic Powder
- 1 Tbsp of Onion Powder
- 1 Tbsp of Italian Seasoning or choice of herbs
- 1 Tbsp of Char-Griller Lemon Pepper Rub
- 1 Tsp of Cayenne Pepper

Directions:

1. If you prefer to rinse your chicken breasts, do so in cold water. Pat completely dry with paper towels. In a resealable bag add olive oil, and all herbs and seasonings. Add chicken and seal the bag before mixing until all pieces are thoroughly coated. Place the bag(s) in the refrigerator for 1

hour-overnight. With Flat Iron preheated to medium heat, add chicken breast and generous squirt of water to the cooktop before covering with the Char-Griller Basting Dome. Keeping covered, allow it to cook for 9-10 minutes. Remove Basting Dome and generously squeeze juice from lemon over each chicken breast. Allow chicken to cook uncovered for 5-6 more minutes, letting water to evaporate and slight crusting to form on bottom before flipping once more. Cook chicken until the internal temperature reaches 165°F. Serve immediately. Enjoy!

Roasted Spatchcock Turkey

Cooking Time: 45 Min

Ingredients:

- 12-20 lb. Turkey
- 1½ Tsp. rosemary
- 3 Tbsp. Kosher salt
- ¾ Tsp. pepper
- ¾ Tsp. garlic powder

Directions:

1. Combine rosemary, Kosher salt, pepper and garlic powder in a bowl and mix well. Set aside.
2. Rinse the turkey and pat dry with paper towel. Place turkey breast-side down. Using sharp kitchen shears, cut along both sides of the backbone, beginning at the tail end.
3. Tip: Set aside the backbone and giblets for stock, if desired.
4. Open the turkey, remove any large pieces of fat and break the breastbone.
5. Tip: Place your hand on one side of the breast, close to the breastbone, and push down firmly until you hear a crack. Repeat on the other side.
6. Separate the legs and thighs and loosen the skin from the breast and season the meat with herb mixture from Step 1. Do this by slowly working your fingers between the breast and the skin.
7. Generously butter under the skin and on top of the turkey pieces.
8. Place an aluminum pan underneath the grates to catch drippings and juices. Place the breast on the grill first and allow to roast for 20 minutes at 325°F. Collect the juices from the pan and pour into a small bowl for basting.
9. After 20 minutes, add the legs and thighs. Baste the turkey every 25 minutes.
10. Cook until center of breast meat reaches 165°F and skin is golden brown. Remove from grill and let rest 5-10 minutes before slicing and serving.

Fried Chicken And Corn

Cooking Time: 10 Min

Ingredients:

- 2 C. flour
- 2 oz. corn starch
- 2 oz. paprika
- 1 Tbsp. cinnamon
- Salt & pepper to taste
- 4 ears of corn
- 4 oz. melted unsalted butter
- 1 Tbsp. paprika

Directions:

1. Soak chicken up to 24 hours in buttermilk and hot sauce
2. In a bowl mix corn starch, salt & pepper, cinnamon, and paprika
3. Mix ingredients well
4. Add chicken to mixture and coat thoroughly
5. Once coated, let sit for 30 minutes
6. Heat grill to 375°F

7. In a hot cast iron skillet, add chicken and oil
8. Cook chicken 3-5 minutes per side
9. Soak corn in saltwater for up to 24 hours
10. Boil them in butter water for 10 minutes before adding to grill
11. On a plate, mix paprika, salt, pepper, and melted butter
12. Mix and roll corn and cover with mixture
13. Add to grill and cook for 3-5 minutes

Classic Smoked Spatchcocked Turkey

Ingredients:

- 14 Lb Turkey
- Char-Griller Chicken Rub
- Ghee or Butter

Directions:

1. Preheat offset smoker to between 225 and 250.
2. Tip: You can also do use the AKORN with a Smoking Stone.
3. Add mesquite or hickory chunks to Side Fire Box.
4. Place turkey on a cutting board breast-side down.
5. Using a pair of kitchen shears, cut the backbone out of the turkey.
6. Flip the turkey so the breast-side is up and using two hands, press down on the breastbone until you hear it break and the turkey lies flat on the cutting board.
7. Season the inside and the outside of the turkey with Char-Griller Chicken Rub making sure to rub it into the meat.
8. Place a drip pan under the grates where the turkey will sit.
9. Place the turkey on the grates in the middle of the main barrel of the smoker.
10. Baste turkey with melted ghee every 30 to 45 minutes.
11. Add additional lit charcoal if needed to maintain temperature.
12. The turkey is done when a thermometer reads 165 when interested into the thickest part of the breast.
13. Tip: Turkey will take about 30 to 40 minutes per pound to cook.
14. When turkey reaches 165 degrees, remove from grill and let rest for 20 minutes before carving.

Curried Chicken Skewers

Cooking Time: 10-12 Min

Ingredients:

- 3-4 lb. chicken tenders
- 2 Tbsp. vegetable oil
- 2 Tbsp. yellow mustard
- 2 Tbsp. honey
- 2 Tbsp. curry powder
- 1 Tsp. salt
- ½ Tsp. garlic powder
- ½ Tsp. pepper
- ½ Tsp. allspice

Directions:

1. Soak the bamboo skewers in water for 15 minutes, so they don't burn on the grill.
2. While skewers are soaking, rinse the chicken tenders and pat dry with paper towel.
3. Combine oil, mustard, honey, curry powder, garlic powder, allspice, salt and pepper in a medium bowl to make curry seasoning and mix well. Add chicken, turning to coat evenly and skewer.
4. Place skewered chicken tenders on the grill at 375°F for 10 minutes, until internal temperature reaches 165°F.

Smoked Carolina Turkey

Ingredients:

- 10-12 lb. turkey
- 3 Tbsp. red pepper flakes
- ¼ C. paprika
- ¼ C. ground mustard
- ½ C. brown sugar
- 2 Tbsp. coarse black pepper
- 2 Tbsp. Kosher salt
- 2 Tbsp. melted butter

Directions:

1. Pour melted butter over turkey, or use marinade injector to inject butter into turkey
2. Mix red pepper flakes, paprika, ground mustard, brown sugar, black pepper and salt in small bowl to create seasoning mix
3. Rub turkey all over with seasoning mix
4. Place turkey on grill over indirect heat at 250°F or use Smokin' Stone
5. Inject turkey with its own juices every other hour
6. Cook time is 1 hour per pound or until turkey reaches internal temp of 165°F

SEAFOOD

Fish And Chips

Cooking Time: 12 Min

Ingredients:

- 4 cod filets
- 3-4 Idaho potatoes
- 1 C. flour
- 1 C. milk
- 1 egg
- 1 Tsp. Old Bay seasoning

Directions:

1. Heat grill to 350-400°F.
2. Let oil heat up in skillet until it sizzles when splashed with a few drops of water.
3. 3-4 Idaho potatoes with skin on, cut into french fries.
4. Let them soak in water for 20-30 minutes to remove excess starch.
5. Pat dry on paper towels before frying.
6. Fries are done when they begin to turn golden
7. Mix batter until only a few clumps of flour remain. Don't over mix.
8. Dredge fish in flour seasoned in Old Bay, if you prefer, before dipping in batter
9. Let fish filets fry on each side for 2-3 minutes, until golden crispy brown.
10. Serve with coleslaw and tartar sauce. Delicious!

Grilled Coconut Lime Foil Packets

Cooking Time: 12 To 15 Min

Ingredients:

- 1 Small, Yellow Onion - Chopped
- 3 Garlic Cloves
- Shredded Sweetened Coconut - 1 Cup
- Zest and Juice from 1 Lime
- Fresh Cilantro - 1 Cup
- Extra Virgin Olive Oil - 1/4 Cup
- Soy Sauce - 1/4 Cup
- Raw Shrimp, Peeled and Deveined - 1 Pound
- Corn Kernels - 2 Cups
- 1 Zucchini - Sliced into 1/4 inch rounds and halved
- Halved Cherry Tomatoes - 1 Cup
- Salt and Pepper to Taste
- Fajita Seasoning - 1 tsp

Directions:

1. Using a blender, combine onion, garlic, coconut, lime zest, lime juice, cilantro, olive oil, and soy sauce. Blend until smooth.
2. Place marinade and shrimp in a bowl and toss to coat.
3. Set aside for 5 minutes.
4. Preheat grill to medium high heat.
5. Tear off four large squares of foil.
6. Spray one side of foil with cooking spray.
7. Divide vegetables and shrimp evenly among each packet.
8. Season with salt, pepper and fajita seasoning.
9. Foil up packets and seal completely.
10. Put packets on grill, close the lid, and grill for 6 minutes. Turn packets over and grill for 7 minutes.
11. Open packets and stir.
12. Sprinkle with fresh cilantro and serve.

Honey Sriracha Lime Salmon

Cooking Time: 25 Min

Ingredients:

- 1 Lb Salmon
- 1 Tsp Kosher Salt
- 1/2 Tsp Coarse Black Pepper
- 1/2 Tsp Garlic Powder
- 1 Tsp Olive Oil
- 1/4 Cup Sriracha
- 1/4 Cup Honey
- 2 Garlic Cloves (Minced)
- 1 Lime

Directions:

1. Coat salmon with a light layer of olive oil on both sides. Lightly season with salt, pepper, and garlic powder.
2. Heat grill to 325 F. Place salmon skin side down indirectly from the heat once the grill has reached the targeted temp.
3. In a heat safe bowl combine sriracha, honey, minced garlic, and lime. Bring the mixture to a boil and reduce heat to let simmer. Once salmon has reached an internal temp between 140F - 142F apply a layer of the sauce mixture to the top of the salmon.
4. Once salmon has reached an internal temp of 145 F pull from grill. Garnish with an extra squeeze of lime and cilantro. Serve and enjoy!

Grilled Swordfish With Lemon-caper Sauce

Ingredients:

- 8oz. swordfish steaks
- 4 oz. jar capers, drained
- ½ C. mayonnaise
- ½ C. sour cream
- 1½ fresh lemons, juiced
- ½ Tsp. seasoned salt
- ¾ Tsp. white pepper
- 1 Tsp. dried minced onion
- 5 Tbsp. green onion tops, minced (optional, for garnish)

Directions:

1. Blend all ingredients, except green onion tops.
2. Transfer to bowl, cover with plastic wrap and refrigerate for 1 hour.
3. Swordfish
4. Season swordfish steaks on both sides with seasoned salt, to taste.
5. Place on the grill at 400°F for 10 minutes per side. Swordfish is ready when the internal temperature reaches 140°F.
6. Remove the fish and let it rest for 5-10 minutes before serving.
7. Sauce swordfish steaks with lemon-caper sauce and garnish with green onion tops.

Buffalo Lemon Shrimp

Cooking Time: 12 Min

Ingredients:

- Raw Shrimp, Peeled and Deveined - 1 Pound
- Hot Sauce (I Use Buffalo Sauce for this Recipe) - 3 Tablespoons
- Minced Garlic - 1 Tablespoon
- Olive Oil - 2 Tablespoons
- Juiced Lemon - 1
- Lemon Cut Into Wedges for Serving - 1
- Salt to Taste

Directions:

1. Taking advantage of seasonal ingredients is the name of the game, so for the remainder of the summer, chicken wings are going to have to move aside. If you haven't been grilling shrimp this

season, now is the time. She loves to use charcoal for this recipe, as shrimp cook quickly and charcoal flame provides so much flavor in such a short amount of time. Let's dig in!

2. Light your charcoal in your chimney and wait until the bricks are glowing red and ashy around the edges. Dump under the grates of your Char-Griller Grill, and close the lid, letting the grates heat for 5-10 minutes.

3. While grill is heating, toss shrimp with buffalo sauce, minced garlic, the juice of one lemon, olive oil, and plenty of salt. Let marinate on the counter for a few minutes.

4. Once the grill is heated, spray the grates with non-stick spray, and lay your shrimp and lemon wedges out to cook. Grill on each side for 2 minutes, until some deep char marks form, and they are curled up and a beautiful vibrant pink color.

5. Serve on a large tray with grilled lemon wedges and an extra sprinkle of salt! These are super delicious on a salad, in a taco, or as the main dish at your next barbecue! Happy Grilling.

Cedar Plank Smoked Salmon

Cooking Time: 1-1.5 Hrs

Ingredients:

- Salmon fillets
- 1/3 C. olive oil
- 1/3 C. soy sauce
- 1/3 C. maple syrup
- ½ Tsp. cayenne pepper

Directions:

1. Rinse salmon and pat dry with paper towel. 2. Mix all ingredients together and pour evenly over salmon in an airtight container. Reserve some for basting and set aside. 3. Place in refrigerator and allow to marinate for 1 hour, or longer if desired. 4. Pre-heat grill to 275°F. Soak cedar planks in water for 3 minutes before placing on the grill to warm for 5-10 minutes. 5. Place salmon on cedar planks and smoke until the internal temperature of the fish reaches 145°F, basting with reserved marinade every 30 minutes.

2. Remove from grill and serve. Enjoy!

Flavor Pro Cedar Plank Salmon

Cooking Time: 25 Min

Ingredients:

- 2 Cedar Planks
- 2 Salmon Filets
- Olive Oil
- Rosemary
- Salt and Pepper to Taste

Directions:

1. Soak cedar planks in water for at least 8 hours. Set up the Flavor Pro for Indirect cooking Add 30 to 40 charcoal briquettes to one side of the flavor drawer Ignite charcoal with gas burners set to medium high Once charcoal is lit, turn off gas burners and allow to fully ash over Rub salmon on both sides with olive oil. Season with salt and pepper, rosemary sprigs and slices of lemon Place Salmon on the side of the grill away from the charcoal Cook salmon for 15 minutes or until flakey.

Grilled Seafood Boil

Cooking Time: 20-25 Min

Ingredients:

- 2 Lb. Of Large Shrimp, Deveined and Peeled, Remove the tails during prep if you prefer
- 2 Andouille Sausages (Thinly Sliced)

- 2 Large Ears Of Corn, Shucked and Each Cut Into 4 Small Cobs
- 1 Lb. of Red Bliss potatoes (Cut Into Small Cubes)
- 1 Lemon (Sliced Into 4 Wedges)
- 4 Tbsp of Butter
- 4 Tsp of Char-Griller "Creole" Rub
- 4 Tsp Of Italian Seasoning
- 4 Tsp Of Minced Garlic
- Extra Virgin Olive Oil
- Salt and Pepper To Taste

Directions:

1. Preheat your grill to medium-high heat. Arrange 4 pieces of aluminum foil, about 1 foot long for each packet. Evenly divide shrimp, sausages, corn, potatoes and lemon amongst each "packet". Drizzle each packet with olive oil, 1 tsp of garlic, salt and pepper, and 1 tsp of Char-Griller's Creole seasoning. Use hands to mix to ensure all elements are coated evenly. Top each off packet with 1 tsp of Italian Seasoning, and 1 Tbsp of butter. Fold each packet, ensuring the entire mixture is covered and twist the edges seal it closed. Place the foil packets directly on the grill and cook for 20-25 minutes or until they are cooked to your liking. Serve warm, enjoy!

Oysters "dougie-feller"

Cooking Time: 15 Min

Ingredients:

- 10-12 Large Oysters
- 2 oz. pancetta
- 2-3 Tbsp. shallot, chopped
- 2 Tbsp. unsalted butter
- 4 cloves minced garlic
- 3 Tbsp. hot pepper sauce
- 2 oz. panko crumbs
- Juice of ½ lemon
- 2 C. spinach, chopped
- Bed of rock salt

Directions:

1. Shuck oysters
2. Melt 2 Tbsp. unsalted butter in cast iron skillet
3. Sauté pancetta in skillet until crispy (5-7 minutes)
4. Add chopped shallot, and cook until fragrant, about 1 minute
5. Add 4 cloves minced garlic, cook until fragrant, about 1 minute
6. Add 3 Tbsp. hot pepper sauce, stir to incorporate
7. Mix in chopped spinach
8. Sauté until spinach begins to wilt
9. Add 2 oz of panko crumbs
10. Season with salt and pepper to taste
11. Stir in lemon juice
12. Remove from heat and set aside
13. Place 10-12 large oysters on grill at 350°F, shell side up, cooking for 5-7 minutes
14. Remove from grill and lay oysters on a bed of rock salt
15. Top oysters with pancetta and spinach mixture

Steamed Mussels With Pancetta

Cooking Time: 30 Min

Ingredients:

- 2 lbs. fresh mussels, scrubbed and de-bearded
- 4 oz. pancetta, diced
- 3/4 C. dry white wine
- 2 Tbsp. olive oil
- 1/2 onion, diced
- 4 cloves garlic, peeled and minced

- 1 1/4 C. fish stock
- 2 Tbsp. lemon juice
- 2 Tbsp. chives, minced
- 8-10 grape tomatoes, sliced lengthwise
- Pinch of crushed red pepper flakes
- Salt and pepper to taste
- French bread, sliced and toasted for serving

Directions:

1. Add pancetta from Step 1 and mussels to pan and allow to steam with lid closed, until mussels have opened, about 5-10 minutes.
2. Open grill lid and stir in dry white wine, fish stock, lemon juice, chives, sliced tomatoes and crushed red pepper flakes, if desired, and season with salt and pepper, to taste. Simmer for 3-5 minutes until almost all of the liquid is evaporated.
3. Remove pan from the heat and discard any shells that do not open. Serve with toasted French bread. Enjoy!

Creole Blackened Salmon

Cooking Time: 10 Min

Ingredients:

- 1 Salmon Filet
- Avocado Oil
- Char-Griller Creole Seasoning

Directions:

1. Preheat grill to 400F
2. Slice salmon filet into approx 3" portions.
3. Lightly coat portions in avocado oil and season using Creole seasoning.
4. Place salmon on grill (I like to use copper grill mats for fish) grill approx 5-6 minutes, flip salmon and grill another 3-4 minutes.
5. Remove and enjoy!!

Gravity 980 Grilled Lobster Tails

Cooking Time: 10 Min

Ingredients:

- 6 Lobster Tails
- 1/3 Cup of Melted Butter
- 1 Tbsp OF Extra Virgin Olive Oil
- 1 Lemon
- 1 Tbsp of Parsley
- 1 Tbsp of Chives
- 1 Tbsp of Minced Garlic
- 1 Tbsp of Char-Griller Creole Rub
- 1/2 Tsp of Salt
- 1/2 Tsp of Pepper

Directions:

1. To prep lobster tails, using kitchen shears, cut the top of the shell lengthwise down the middle. Using a sharp knife, cut through this slit, halfway through the flesh, excluding the very tip of the tail. Flatten each tail so the shell opens around the meat. Place a skewer through each tail to prevent it from curling during cooking. In a bowl, combine butter, parsley, ½ the chives, minced garlic and Creole rub. Line tails on a baking sheet and brush each lightly with oil, salt and pepper. Remove the fire shutter from your Gravity 980, load and light the hopper then set to 350°F. Place the lobster tails, flesh side down on the grill and allow to cook for 5 minutes. Flip each tail over and drizzle the tops generously with garlic butter mixture. Grill for additional 5 minutes or until lobster becomes fully cooked. Sprinkle finished lobster tails with remaining chives and serve with lemon wedges. Enjoy!

Rosemary Shrimp Skewers

Cooking Time: 5 Min

Ingredients:

- Shrimp Seasoned with Salt, Pepper, and Jerk Seasoning - 1 Pound
- Fresh Rosemary - Use full stalk and remove half of leaves to expose the stalk, this becomes your skewer

Directions:

1. Skewer two shrimp per skewer
2. Cook on grill at 350 degrees, 5 minutes per side till cooked thoroughly

Fresh Garlic Parsley Butter Salmon

Cooking Time: 30 Min

Ingredients:

- Garlic Parsley Butter
- 2 (6 oz) Salmon Mignons
- Tajin to Taste
- Dry Parsley Flakes to Taste
- Olive Oil

Directions:

1. Make Garlic Parsley Butter
2. Add Tajin seasoning to butter to taste or use favorite seafood seasoning.
3. Add 1 tbsp. of Fresh Garlic Parsley to each salmon mignons patty.
4. Add dry parsley flakes to taste.
5. Preheat your Char-griller Premium Red Kettle 14822 to 350°.
6. Insert the Char-griller Chimney in the middle of the grill in the fire pit area and do not remove it and no need to release the coals.
7. The handle will not melt inside the Premium Kettles. This will give you a hot fire in the middle of the grill for easy cast iron cooking and also raises the charcoal. The middle small grill grate can be easily moved with a Char-griller grate lifter to add charcoal.
8. Add olive oil to your cast iron skillet: just enough to coat the bottom of the skillet and place over the fire to preheat.
9. Then place the salmon on the cast iron skillet.
10. Flip Salomon after 12 minutes and toss the melted fresh garlic parsley on all sides of the salmon using a spoon.
11. Add 2 additional tbsp. to the skillet for extra flavor.
12. Then move the cast iron skillet away from the middle of the grill for a quick offset cook for 15 minutes.Tip: Continuously add the melted fresh garlic parsley on all sides of the salmon using a spoon for extra flavor.
13. Enjoy!

Shrimp Tacos

Cooking Time: 20 Min

Ingredients:

- 2 Lbs of Shrimp (Tail off, Peeled,and Deveined Shrimp)
- Jalapeno-Lime Seasoning
- Tequila Lime Marinade
- 1 Head Green Cabbage
- 3-4 Jalapenos
- 1 Bundle Cilantro
- White Onion
- Green Onion
- Lime (Zest and Juice)
- Coleslaw Dressing
- 2 Tbsp Sriracha Hot Sauce
- 16 Oz Sour Cream
- Corn Tortillas

Directions:

1. Prep shrimp by removing shell, tail, and devein if this is not already done
2. Season and marinate with Jalapeno-Lime Seasoning and Tequila-Lime Marinade Shred green cabbage and add to large mixing bowl
3. Remove seeds and Julianne jalapenos
4. Chop cilantro and green onions and add to the mixing bowl
5. Add zest and juice from 1 lime
6. Season coleslaw with Jalapeno-Lime seasoning
7. Add coleslaw dressing and mix all together
8. Dice white onion and set aside for taco topping
9. In a separate mixing bowl combine sour cream, Sriracha, Tequila-Lime Marinade, and Jalapeno-Lime seasoning
10. Preheat your grill and cast iron skillet
11. Cook shrimp hot and fast in a cast iron skillet
12. Char tortillas directly on the grill
13. Assemble tacos and enjoy!
14. Pitt Tips:Fresh shrimp is always best, but frozen shrimp works perfectly fine also! NEVER microwave your tortillas!

Grilled Lobster Tails

Cooking Time: 10 Min

Ingredients:

- 8oz. lobster tails
- 2 sticks salted butter
- 1 Tbsp. garlic

Directions:

1. Butterfly the lobster. To do this, use a sharp knife or kitchen shears to split the lobster shell all the way to the tail. Slice the meat in half along the cut line on the shell, being careful not to slice through the lobster. Open the lobster shell-side down and lay it flat. 2. To make clarified butter, melt butter in a pan. Bring to a boil and reduce to a simmer. Skim the foam from the surface. Strain the butter to further remove residue, if desired. Add garlic and stir to combine. Pour into a small bowl and set aside to keep warm. 3. Brush lobster tails with clarified garlic butter and place on the grill, shell-side up, at 400°F for 3-4 minutes. Flip and grill for another 5-6 minutes. Lobster is done when internal temperature reaches 135°F.

Spicy Crawfish Dip

Cooking Time: 15 Min

Ingredients:

- ½ C. butter
- ½ C. chopped bell pepper
- ½ C. chopped onion (or green onion)
- 1 Tbsp. basil
- 2 cloves minced garlic
- 2 Tsp. Old bay or Cajun seasoning
- Salt and pepper, to taste
- 1 lb. pack frozen, cooked, peeled crawfish tails, thawed and undrained
- 8 oz. cream cheese, softened
- Sriracha, to taste

Directions:

1. Pre-heat grill to 350°F and add Smokin' Stone under the grates. Place a cast iron skillet on top of the grates and heat until very hot.
2. Add butter to skillet and allow to melt. Add bell pepper and onion. Sauté for 2 minutes, stirring occasionally.
3. Add basil, garlic, seasoning and salt and pepper to taste and stir. Add crawfish and stir to combine.

4. Stir in cream cheese until mixture is smooth. Stir in Sriracha sauce, to taste and allow to smoke for 10 minutes with lid closed at 350°F.

5. Remove from grill and serve with crackers or toasted French bread slices. Enjoy!

Spicy Caribbean Shrimp

Cooking Time: 6-8 Min

Ingredients:

- 2 lbs. large shrimp, peeled and deveined
- Pineapple cubes
- 2 C. pineapple juice
- ½ C. coconut milk
- ¼ C. dark rum
- 4 habanero peppers, cored and seeded
- 2 Tsp. lime juice
- Your favorite jerk seasoning, to taste

Directions:

1. Pre-heat grill to 400°F. Combine pineapple juice, coconut milk, dark rum, habanero peppers and lime juice in a blender and mix well. Place shrimp and pineapple cubes on to bamboo skewers and add marinade. Marinate in the refrigerator no longer than 30 minutes in a non-reactive pan, i.e. ceramic or glass. The acid from the lime juice and pineapple juice will cook the shrimp (like in a ceviche) if left in longer. Remove shrimp skewers from marinade and season to taste on both sides with jerk seasoning. Discard marinade. Cook 3-4 minutes per side at 400°F, until shrimp is pink and opaque.
2. Remove from grill and serve!

2-burner Flat Iron Easy Shrimp Tacos

Cooking Time: 10 Min

Ingredients:

- 1 Lb. of medium-sized shrimp, deveined and peeled with tails removed
- 6-8 Flour or Corn Tortillas
- 1 Tbsp of Extra Virgin Olive Oil
- 1 Tbsp of Char-Griller Chili Lime or Taco & Fajita Rub
- 1/2 Tbsp of Garlic Powder
- 1/2 Tbsp of Onion Powder
- 1/2 Tbsp of Pepper
- A Dash of Salt
- Optional Toppings: Iceberg Lettuce, Sour Cream, Tomatoes, Cilantro, Salsa, Avocado

Directions:

1. Make these simple shrimp tacos as complex or as stuffed as you'd like. Our Rubs will take this dish to the next level, preparing it perfectly for whatever your taste buds have in mind.
2. Prep shrimp, by drying as much as possible with paper towels. In a bowl, combine shrimp with olive oil and all seasonings. With Flat Iron preheated to medium-high heat, add shrimp to cooktop and cook while occasionally stirring for about 5-6 minutes or until shrimp are no longer pink. Remove from Flat Iron. Add tortillas to the cooktop and warm up, cooking for 2-3 minutes per side. Assemble the tacos with desired toppings and serve immediately. Enjoy!

Seared Scallops With Pancetta

Cooking Time: 15 Min

Ingredients:

- 12 U-10 Scallops
- 4 oz. pancetta, chopped
- ½ red onion or 1 shallot, minced
- 2 C. green peas, drained and divided
- 4 oz. Parmesan cheese

- 1 Tbsp. olive oil
- Juice of 1 lemon
- 4 oz. mint, divided
- Salt and pepper, to taste

Directions:

1. Pre-heat grill to 375°F. Fry pancetta in a cast iron pan for about 5 minutes and drain grease. Add minced red onion (or shallot, if substituting) and 1 C. peas to pan and season with salt and pepper, then add ½ of mint and stir to incorporate. Cook until warmed through. 2. Combine 1 C. peas and lemon juice, remaining mint, olive oil and Parmesan cheese in a food processor. Season to taste with salt and pepper and blend until smooth. 3. Rinse scallops and pat dry with paper towel. Season scallops with salt and pepper to taste on all sides. Place on the grill and sear for 3-5 minutes per side.
2. To serve, spoon peas onto plate, add scallops and top with pancetta mixture. Enjoy!

Grilled Salmon

Cooking Time: 20 Min

Ingredients:

- 4 Salmon Fillets
- 1/4 Cup of Olive Oil
- 2 Tbsp of Char-Griller Creole Seasoning
- 1/2 Tbsp of Garlic Powder
- 1 Tsp of Dried Parsley
- Kosher Salt
- Ground Black Pepper
- 4 Lemon Wedges

Directions:

1. Generously coat the salmon with olive oil and all seasonings. Heat your grill to medium-high heat. Add salmon fillets, flesh side down, cooking for 6-8 minutes with the grill closed. Once the meat is firm enough, flip it over, closing the lid, cooking for an additional 3-8 minutes depending on desired doneness. Remove from heat and allow the fillets to rest for 5 minutes before removing the skin and serving with lemon wedges along with any desired condiments and toppings.

Shrimp 'n Grits

Cooking Time: 20-25 Min

Ingredients:

- 1 lb. shrimp, peeled and deveined
- Original All-Purpose BBQ rub, to taste, or preferred rub
- ½ red bell pepper, chopped
- ½ onion, chopped
- Handful of cilantro, chopped
- 4 C. water
- 1 Tsp. salt
- 1 C. stone-ground grits
- 2-3 Tbsp. butter
- 4 oz. heavy cream
- 2 oz. Parmesan cheese
- Salt and pepper, to taste

Directions:

1. Pre-heat grill to 375°F. Bring water to a boil, add grits and cook until water is absorbed, about 20- 25 minutes. Remove from heat, stir in butter, cheese and heavy cream. Add salt and pepper, to taste and stir. Set aside. 2. While grits are cooking, melt butter in skillet and sauté red pepper and onions until soft, about 5-7 minutes, stirring occasionally. 3. Add shrimp and season with Original All-Purpose BBQ Rub and cook for 3-5 minutes, until opaque and fully cooked. Add cilantro and salt and pepper, to taste and stir to combine.
2. To serve, spoon grits into bowls and top with shrimp and red pepper mixture. Garnish with more cilantro and enjoy!

Grilled Tilapia

Cooking Time: 15-20 Min

Ingredients:

- 3 whole Tilapia
- 2 oz. smoked paprika
- 2 oz. Old Bay seasoning
- Salt and pepper, to taste
- Chopped parsley
- Olive oil
- 4 garlic cloves thinly sliced

Directions:

1. Set up grill for indirect heat and preheat to 350°F.
2. While grill is heating, stuff the inside of each fish with chopped parsley and garlic, then season inside and out with smoked paprika and Old Bay seasoning. Drizzle with olive oil and top with more parsley, smoked paprika/seasoning mix and remaining garlic.
3. Place fish on the grill oiled side down and drizzle with more oil and season with remaining parsley, smoked paprika/seasoning mix. Allow fish to cook for 7-10 minutes on each side.
4. Enjoy!

Lobster Roll

Cooking Time: 10 Min

Ingredients:

- 8 oz. lobster tails
- ½ C. mayonnaise
- 3 Tbsp. lemon juice
- 2 celery stalks, finely chopped
- 2 Tbsp. fresh parsley leaves, chopped
- 4 rolls, split and lightly toasted
- Melted butter, for brushing
- Salt and pepper, to taste

Directions:

1. Brush lobster with butter and place on the grill, shell-side up, at 400°F for 3-4 minutes. Flip and grill for another 5-6 minutes. Lobster is done when internal temperature reaches 135°F.
2. While lobster is grilling, stir together mayonnaise, lemon juice, celery, parsley in a large bowl and add salt and pepper, to taste.
3. When lobster has cooled, scoop meat from shells and roughly chop. Fold into mayonnaise mixture from Step
4. Butter both sides of rolls and fill with lobster mixture. Enjoy!

Lemon Pepper Shrimp

Cooking Time: 7 Min

Ingredients:

- 1.5 lbs Peel-n-Eat Shrimp
- 1 Tbsp Avocado Oil
- 1/2 Stick Butter, Melted
- 1/2 Tbsp Black Pepper
- 1 Tbsp Lemon Zest
- 1 Tbsp Minced Garlic
- 1 Tbsp Parsley, Chopped
- 1/2 Tbsp Salt

Directions:

1. Fill your chimney with charcoal, and light over side burner flame until coals are lit. Allow them to burn for 20-30 minutes, then release into grill and close lid, allowing grates to heat to high temp.
2. Toss shrimp in avocado oil, and scatter on grill. Close the lid and let shrimp cook 3-5 minutes, until pink and charred. Remove from heat
3. Mix butter with pepper, lemon juice & zest, garlic, salt, and parsley. Toss the hot grilled shrimp in sauce, and serve immediately with tons of napkins! Enjoy!

Lobster Mac 'n Cheese

Cooking Time: 30-35 Min

Ingredients:

- 8oz. lobster tails
- 1 lb. Cavatappi or elbow macaroni
- 1 qt. milk
- 1 stick unsalted butter, divided
- ½ C. all-purpose flour
- 12 oz. Gruyere cheese, grated
- 8 oz. extra-sharp Cheddar, grated
- 1½ C. breadcrumbs
- ½ Tsp. black pepper
- ½ Tsp. nutmeg
- Kosher salt, to taste

Directions:

1. Butterfly the lobster. To do this, use a sharp knife or kitchen shears to split the lobster shell all the way to the tail. Slice the meat in half along the cut line on the shell, being careful not to slice through the lobster. Open the lobster shell-side down, lay it flat and brush with butter. 2. Place lobster on the grill, meat side down at 375°F for 4-5 minutes. Flip and grill for another 6-7 minutes. 3. While lobster is grilling, make the Mac 'n cheese. Lobster is done when internal temperature reaches 135°F. 4. Remove lobster from grill and allow to cool. Scoop meat from shells and roughly chop.

2. Mac 'n cheese

3. Pour oil into a large pot of boiling salted water. Add pasta and cook according to package directions, 6-8 minutes. Drain well. 2. Meanwhile, heat the milk in a small saucepan until hot, being careful not to boil it. Whisk together 6 Tbsp. butter and flour in a large pot. Add hot milk and cook for 1-2 minutes, until thickened and smooth. Remove from heat and add cheese, 1 Tbsp. salt, pepper, and nutmeg. Add cooked macaroni and lobster and stir well. Spoon mixture into cast iron pan. 4. Melt the remaining butter, stir in breadcrumbs and sprinkle on top. Place pan on the grill at 375°F and bake for 30- 35 minutes, or until the sauce is bubbly and the macaroni is lightly browned on top.

Cedar Plank Salmon

Cooking Time: 20-25 Min

Ingredients:

- Whole Coho Salmon 2 Lbs
- Cedar Plank Boards
- Olive Oil
- Kary's Roux All Purpose Seasoning
- Caribeque Lemon Garlic Seasoning
- Lemons
- Dill
- Parsley
- Asparagus (Optional)
- Garlic Parsley Butter

Directions:

1. Soak the cedar plank boards in water for one hour prior to prepping the salmon. Slice the whole salmon into four fillets, it is fine to leave the skin on. Place the salmon fillets on the cedar plank boards with a few lemon slices and asparagus.Tip: Apply olive oil directly on the cedar plank side you place the salmon to keep it from sticking.

2. Apply even coat of olive oil to the top/sides of the salmon fillets. Apply Caribeque Lemon Garlic Seasoning and Kary's Roux All Purpose Seasoning: use to taste. Add Garlic Parsley Butter to the top of each salmon: 1tsp per fillet. Add dill, parsley and additional lemons to

the salmon fillets. Sprinkle parsley flakes when done to complete the prepping process.

3. Grilling directions: 20-25 minutes, internal temperature 145°

4. Preheat your grill to 400° Add cedar planks with the salmon to the grill directly over the lump Charcoal. No need to rotate, allow the grill, charcoal and cedar plank salmon to roast the salmon. Tip: It's also okay if your temperature drops: check out the recipe video on YouTube full for temperature control tips. Cook to internal temperature 145° and remove the cedar planks from the

5. Grill and it's ready for immediate eating.Tip: take the guesswork out and use the Char-Griller Grills folding probe to easily see what temperature the salon is at. Enjoy!

Seared Sesame Ahi Tuna

Cooking Time: 20 Min

Ingredients:

- 2 Ahi Tuna steaks
- 2 Tbsp. olive oil
- 1 Tsp. sesame oil
- 3 Tbsp. black sesame seeds
- 3 Tbsp. white sesame seeds
- Salt and pepper, to taste
- Wasabi, for serving
- Lemon wedges, for serving
- Soy sauce, for serving

Directions:

1. Pre-heat grill to 400°F. Rinse tuna steaks and pat dry with paper towel. Place steaks on a clean cutting board and coat with olive oil and 1 Tsp. of sesame oil. Season on both sides with salt and pepper, to taste. 2. Toss black and white sesame seeds together in a large bowl and season with salt and pepper, to taste. Press the tuna steaks into the sesame seeds, covering all sides of the steaks. 3. Place the steaks on the grill to sear for 2 minutes on each side, flipping halfway through. Watch the steaks closely so that the sesame seeds don't burn. Use tongs to lift and sear the edges of the steaks. 4. Remove steaks from the grill and allow to rest for 5-10 minutes. Slice the steaks against the grain into 1" thick strips. The steaks should have a rare, bright-red middle.

2. Serve with wasabi, soy sauce and lemon wedges, if desired.

3. Allergy notice: Recipe contains sesame seeds and sesame oil.

Honey-bourbon Glazed Salmon

Cooking Time: 45-60 Min

Ingredients:

- 1 Cedar Plank
- 1 Wild Salmon Filet
- 1 Lemon, sliced
- Lemon pepper seasoning (to taste)
- ½ C. Bourbon
- Water (enough to cover the cedar plank)
- 3 Tbsp. Honey
- 1 oz. Bourbon
- 1 Tsp. Lemon Zest

Directions:

1. Remove the pin bones from the salmon filet with fish bone tweezers. Pour water and bourbon into a large baking dish and soak cedar plank for a minimum of 1 hour.

2. Place salmon filet on cedar plank, sprinkle with lemon pepper seasoning, to taste, and cover with sliced lemons.

3. Prepare the grill for offset smoking by adding citrus wood chunks to the Side Fire Box. Place

the salmon on the grill and smoke at 250° - 275°F for approximately 45 - 60 minutes.

4. Mix the honey, bourbon and lemon zest together in a bowl to make the glaze. After 30 minutes, intermittently brush the honey/bourbon glaze on the salmon.

5. Enjoy the deliciousness!

Blackened Catfish

Cooking Time: 15 Min

Ingredients:

- 4-6 Catfish Filets
- 3-4 Tbsp of Blackening Seasoning (Few Of My Favorites, Mis Rubins Fish Magic, Ashman Bayou Blackening, Pappys Lemon Pepper)
- 2 Tbsp Avocado Oil

Directions:

1. Preheat grill to 450F, I like to use a copper grill mat when grilling fish, works very well. Coat filets with oil and season. Place fish on grill mat, grill 6-8 minutes until you get desired blackened look, flip fish and cook another 3-4 minutes. Remove catfish from grill serve over rice and enjoy!

Bacon Wrapped Seafood Stuffed Shrimp

Cooking Time: 20 Min

Ingredients:

- 2 lbs. jumbo shrimp, deveined and butterflied
- 1 lb. Applewood smoked bacon strips, cut in half
- 1lb. lobster tail meat and/or lump crab meat, cooked and chopped
- 2 Tbsp. butter, melted
- 1 medium yellow pepper, chopped
- 1 small green pepper, chopped
- 1 medium sweet onion, chopped
- 2 Tbsp. fresh garlic, minced
- ¼ C. mayonnaise
- 1 Tbsp. horseradish mustard
- 1 egg, beaten
- 2 Tbsp. seafood all-purpose sauce
- 1 Tsp. seasoned salt
- 1 Tsp. white pepper
- 1 Tsp. garlic powder
- 1 Tsp. onion powder
- 2 Tsp. Chipotle chili powder
- 1 C. cheese crackers, crushed

Directions:

1. Melt butter in a large cast iron skillet and sauté onion, peppers and garlic until tender, 5-7 minutes.
2. Allow to cool and then gradually fold in the remaining ingredients, except shrimp, to seafood mixture from Step 1.
3. Mound 1-2 Tbsp. of stuffing mixture onto shrimp, wrap with ½ strip of bacon and secure with toothpick.
4. Place bacon wrapped shrimp on a metal tray onto the indirect side of the grill at 375°F for 20 minutes.

Grilled Chilean Sea Bass

Cooking Time: 30 Min

Ingredients:

- Whole Chilean Sea bass
- 2 oz. parsley, chopped
- 1½ oz. Original All-Purpose BBQ Rub or your favorite seafood seasoning
- 2 lemons, sliced
- 2-3 sprigs of dill
- Salt and pepper, to taste

- 4 oz. olive oil

Directions:

1. Pre-heat grill to 350°F. Place the charcoal on one side for indirect heat.
2. Score fish diagonally on each side in the thickest part of the meat.
3. Stuff the inside cavity with dill sprigs and lemon slices.
4. Season both sides of the outside of the fish to taste with olive oil, salt and pepper and top with an even layer of Original All-Purpose BBQ Rub, or use your favorite seafood seasoning, and parsley.
5. Lay the fish on the grill for 5-7 minutes on direct heat, then move to the indirect heat side for 15-20 minutes.

DESSERTS

Salted Caramel Chocolate Tart

Cooking Time: 20 Min

Ingredients:

- 1- 8 oz Bag of Sea Salt Kettle Potato Chips, Crushed (Crust)
- 1/4 Cup Flour (Crust)
- 5 Tbsp Unsalted Butter, Melted (Crust)
- 1 Cup Sugar (Caramel)
- 1/2 Cup Heavy Cream (Caramel)
- 6 Tbsp Unsalted Butter (Caramel)
- 1 tsp Sea Salt (Caramel)
- 10 Oz Semisweet Chocolate Chips (Chocolate Layer)
- 1/4 Cup Heavy Cream (Chocolate Layer)
- 1/4 Cup Sugar (Chocolate Layer)
- 2 tsp Vanilla Extract (Chocolate Layer)
- 2 Large Eggs (Chocolate Layer)

Directions:

1. Light grill for indirect heat and heat to 350.
2. In a large bowl, combine crushed chips, melted butter, and flour. Mix until combined.
3. Press into tart pan and place on grill. Bake for 15 minutes.
4. Remove from grill and allow to cool.
5. In a sauce pan over medium heat, add sugar and allow to melt completely, stirring frequently.
6. Add cream and butter, stir until combined.
7. Add sea salt and allow to boil for 5 minutes.
8. Remove from heat and allow to cool for 15 minutes.
9. Pour caramel onto crust.
10. In a saucepan over medium heat, add cream and allow to heat up.
11. Add chocolate chips and sugar, stir until melted and smooth.
12. Add eggs one at a time stirring until combined.
13. Add vanilla and stir.
14. Pour chocolate until crust.
15. Place tart on grill and allow to bake for 20 minutes.
16. Remove from grill and let cool.

Grilled S'mores 4 Ways

Servings: 4

Cooking Time: 5 Min

Ingredients:

- Graham Crackers - 4 Full Crackers
- Large Marshmallows - 4
- Milk Chocolate Bar
- Dark Chocolate Bar
- Cookie Butter
- Peanut and Caramel Candy Bar
- Chili Powder
- Peanut Butter

Directions:

1. Heat grill to 350 degrees
2. Break four graham crackers in half and lay out.
3. Top the first graham cracker with milk chocolate bar and peanut butter.
4. Top the second graham cracker with milk chocolate and cookie butter
5. Top third graham cracker with dark chocolate and a sprinkle of chili powder.
6. Top fourth graham cracker with Snickers Bar cut in half longways.
7. Top each graham cracker with a marshmallow and the other half of the graham cracker.

8. Wrap each s'mores in its own foil packet.
9. Place on warming rack of the grill for 4 to 5 minutes.
10. Enjoy.

Bourbon Glaze For Candied Bacon Scones

Cooking Time: 15 Min

Ingredients:

- Bourbon - 3 Tbsp
- Vanilla - 1 tsp
- Powdered Sugar - 2 cups
- Milk - 4 Tbsp

Directions:

1. Place all ingredients in a small pan and stir to combine. Place pan on grill and allow to heat through for 15 minutes. Stir half way through. Remove from grill and cool. Open grill vents and increase temperature to 400 to cook the scones. Make the scone dough.

Grilled Stuffed Peaches

Cooking Time: 20 Min

Ingredients:

- 1- 2 peaches per person
- 2 Tbsp. honey, divided
- 4 oz. blue cheese, or to taste
- Coarse black pepper, to taste
- 2-3 slices of bacon, for garnish

Directions:

1. Rinse peaches and dry with paper towel. Slice in half, remove stone and cut the pit hole slightly larger.
2. Fry bacon in a pan to desired crispness according to package directions, drain grease and crumble when cool. Set aside in a small bowl.
3. Place peaches cut side down directly on the grill at 350°F for 5-7 minutes, depending on the size.
4. Turn peaches over and fill holes with blue cheese and crumbled bacon and bake for 5-7 minutes, until peaches are softened and cheese is melted.
5. Remove peaches from grill, drizzle with honey and sprinkle with coarse black pepper to serve.

Chocolate Chip Skillet Cookie

Cooking Time: 25-30 Min

Ingredients:

- 2 C. all-purpose flour
- 1 C. butter, melted
- 1 C. brown sugar
- ½ C. sugar
- 2 eggs, beaten
- 1 Tsp. vanilla extract
- 1 Tsp. baking soda
- ½ Tsp. salt
- ¾ C. milk chocolate chunks
- ¾ C. semi-sweet chocolate chips

Directions:

1. Pre-heat grill to 325°F. In a large bowl, combine melted butter and add sugars, stirring until dissolved. 2. Add eggs and vanilla and mix well. 3. Stir in flour, baking soda, and salt. Add in chocolate and stir to combine. 4. Transfer dough into heated cast iron skillet and spread evenly. 5. Bake at 325°F for 25-30 minutes or until the edges are golden brown. The inside will still be slightly gooey.
2. To serve, top with ice cream and eat warm.

Plum Galette

Cooking Time: 45-50 Min

Ingredients:

- 1½ C. and 3 Tbsp. all-purpose flour
- 1 ½ sticks unsalted butter, cut into ½" pieces
- ¼ Tsp. salt
- 1/3 C. ice water
- ¼ C. plus 1/3 C. sugar, reserve 1 Tsp.
- 3 Tbsp. ground almonds
- 2½ lbs. large plums, halved, pitted and cut into ½" wedges
- ½ C. good-quality plum preserves, strained if chunky or seedy
- Corn meal, for dusting

Directions:

1. Put 1½ C. flour, butter and salt into a food processor and mix for 5 seconds. 2. Add ice water and mix for 5 seconds longer, just until the dough holds together. Small pieces of butter should still be visible. 3. Remove the dough and gather it into a ball. On a lightly floured surface, roll out the dough into a large circle, 1/8" thick. 4. Drape the dough over the rolling pin and transfer to a large baking sheet. Refrigerate the dough until firm, 10-20 minutes. 5. While dough is chilling, pre-heat grill to 400°. In a small bowl, combine ¼ C. of the sugar with the ground almonds and 3 Tbsp. flour and mix well. Spread evenly over the dough to within 2" of the edge. 6. Arrange plum wedges on top and dot with butter. Sprinkle 1/3 C. sugar over the fruit. Fold the edge of the dough up over the plums to create a 2" border.

2. Tip: If the dough feels cold and firm when folding up the edges, wait a few minutes until it softens to prevent cracking.

3. Sprinkle the border with the remaining 1 Tsp. sugar. 7. Transfer the galette to a pre-heated pizza stone dusted with corn meal to prevent sticking, and bake at 400°F for 45-50 minutes, until the fruit is very soft and the crust is golden brown. 8. Remove from the grill and evenly brush the preserves over the hot fruit.

4. Allow the galette to cool before slicing and serving. Enjoy!

Glazed Oatmeal Raisin Cookies

Cooking Time: 15 Min

Ingredients:

- 2 C. oats
- 2 C. all-purpose flour
- 1 Tbsp. baking powder
- 2 Tsp. cinnamon
- ½ Tsp. nutmeg
- 1 Tsp. salt
- 2 sticks unsalted butter, softened
- 1 C. sugar
- ½ C. brown sugar
- 2 eggs
- ½ C. raisins
- 1 C. powdered sugar
- 1 Tbsp. vanilla extract
- 2-3 Tbsp. milk

Directions:

1. Pre-heat grill to 350°F. 2. In a medium bowl combine the oats, flour, baking powder, cinnamon, nutmeg, and salt. Mix well and set aside. 3. In a large bowl whisk the butter, sugar, and brown sugar together until sugar is dissolved. Add in the eggs one at a time, stirring well until combined. 4. Add the oat mixture to the butter mixture and stir until combined. Fold in the raisins. 5. Drop 1 Tbsp. of cookie batter onto cookie sheets, 2" apart. Bake 15 minutes or until the edges are golden brown. Remove from grill

and transfer to a wire rack to cool. 6. While cookies are cooling, prepare icing by combining the powdered sugar and vanilla in a bowl. Gradually add in milk until mixture is thick but spreadable.

2. Dunk the top of each cookie into the icing and let the excess drip off. Serve warm.

Candied Bacon Scones With Bourbon Glaze

Cooking Time: 15 Min

Ingredients:

- All Purpose Flour - 3 Cups
- Salt - 3/4 tsp
- Baking Powder - 1 Tbsp
- Sugar - 1/3 cup
- Cinnamon - 1/2 tsp
- Vanilla Extract - 1.5 tsp
- Heavy Cream - 1.5 Cups
- Chopped Bacon - 1/3 cup
- Heavy Cream - 1/4 cup

Directions:

1. Look here for the Candied Bacon Recipe and here for the Bourbon Glaze Recipe.
2. Have the Candied Bacon and Bourbon Glaze Ready nearby. Whisk together flour, salt, baking powder, sugar, and cinnamon. Add 1 1/2 c. cream, vanilla, candied bacon, and stir to combine. Divide dough in half. Flour a cutting board and pat each half into a 6" circle. Brush each circle of dough with the remaining cream. Place dough on parchment paper and cut into 6 triangles. Pull each wedge apart slightly and place in the freezer for 10 minutes. Transfer scones on the parchment paper to the grill grates. Bake for 15 minutes or until golden brown. Remove from grill and allow to cool. Using a 1/4 measuring cup, pour glaze over each scone and top with remaining chopped bacon.

Grilled Pumpkin Pie With Smoked Gingersnap Crust

Cooking Time: 45 To 60 Min

Ingredients:

- 15 Gingersnaps
- 5 Whole Graham Crackers, Broken Apart
- 2 Tbsp Light Brown Sugar
- 4 Tbsp Unsalted Butter, Melted
- 1 - 15 oz Can Pumpkin Puree
- 1 - 14 oz Can of Sweetened Condensed Milk
- 1 Tsp Cinnamon
- 1/2 tsp Ground Ginger
- 1/2 tsp Nutmeg
- 1/2 tsp Ground Cloves
- 2 Eggs, Lightly Beaten

Directions:

1. Add charcoal and a handful of mesquite wood chips to AKORN. Add the Smokin' Stone and preheat to 350 degrees F.
2. Place metal tin of gingersnaps and graham crackers on the grill.
3. Allow the cookies to smoke for 15 minutes.
4. Combine gingersnaps, brown sugar and butter into a food processor and process to moist crumbs.
5. Spoon crumbs into a greased pie pan and press into pan to form crust.
6. Return pie pan to grill and cook for 10 minutes.
7. Remove and allow to cool for 10 minutes.
8. While crust is cooling, whisk together pumpkin, sweetened condensed milk, eggs, and spices until combined.
9. Pour mixture into crust.

10. If desired, place foil around edges of crust to protect it from burning.
11. Return pie to grill and cook for an hour or until a toothpick inserted in the center comes out clean.
12. Cool and serve with whipped cream.

Candy Jar Brownies

Cooking Time: 25 Min

Ingredients:

- 20 Tablespoons Butter (Unsalted)
- 2 Cups White Sugar
- 1 Teaspoon Vanilla
- Four Large Eggs
- 1.5 Cups Unsweetened Cocoa Powder
- 1 Cup All Purpose Flour
- 2 Tablespoons Espresso Powder
- One Tablespoon Salt
- Variety of Candy (About 3 Cups)

Directions:

1. We didn't stop there. We also decided to cook it on the Char-Griller AKORN Kamado Grill because it is so versatile. The chocolate smell plus charcoal...we were in heaven. Before you start, check out our Guide to Baking on the AKORN.
2. Preheat AKORN to 350°F.
3. Cut up a variety of candy bars. Place in individual bowls.
4. Unwrap candy pieces that have foil and add those to individual bowls.
5. In a large bowl, cream together butter and sugar with hand mixer. Mix for 3 minutes.
6. To creamed butter and sugar, add vanilla and eggs. Mix together.
7. Sift four and cocoa into the bowl with the wet ingredients.
8. Add espresso powder and salt. Mix everything together.
9. Note: This mixture will be extremely thick. This is okay. The chocolate from the candy will melt, adding extra moisture to the brownie.
10. Butter baking pan. We used a foil pan so it wouldn't get smoke stains, but any 11 by 9 pan will do.
11. Add 1/3 of the brownie mixture to the bottom of the pan. Spread evenly.
12. Add 1/3 of the candy. (We used the Lava Cake Hersey Kisses and Heath Bar Pieces).
13. Add the second third of the brownie batter. Spread as evenly as you can.
14. Add the second third of the candy. (We used Hersey Cookie Bar and Butterfinger pieces)
15. Add the final layer of brownie batter. Spread evenly.
16. Add the final pieces if candy to decorate the top. (We used Reeses Hearts and M&Ms).
17. Bake on the AKORN for 20 to 25 minutes. Use a toothpick to test if it is done.
18. Cool, cut into pieces and enjoy!
19. Note: Use both the vents to adjust the temperature on the AKRON. More closed vents will help it cool down, open vents will help it heat up. Airflow is key.

Smoked Candied Pecans

Cooking Time: 1 Hrs

Ingredients:

- 1 Lb Pecan Halves
- 3/4 Cup White Sugar
- 1 tsp Ground Cinnamon
- Pinch of Salt
- Pinch of Nutmeg
- 1 Egg White

- 1 Tbsp Water

Directions:

1. Pre-heat Char-Griller smoker to 250 F.
2. In a large bowl whisk together egg white and water until frothy. In a separate bowl combine sugar, ground cinnamon, salt, and nutmeg. Stir until well mixed.
3. Add pecan halves to bowl with the egg white mixture and toss until well coated. Add sugar mixture to the pecans and toss until evenly coated.
4. Place pecans evenly on a baking sheet and smoke at 250 F for one hour or until pecans are evenly browned. Enjoy!

Crème Brûlée

Cooking Time: 30-40 Min

Ingredients:

- 2 C. heavy cream
- 1 Tsp. vanilla extract
- ⅛ Tsp. salt
- 5 egg yolks
- ½ C. sugar, plus more for topping

Directions:

1. Pre-heat grill to 325°F. In a saucepan, combine cream, vanilla extract and salt and cook over low heat just until hot, stirring continuously. Remove from heat and set aside.
2. In a bowl, beat yolks and sugar together until well combined. Add a ¼ C. of the vanilla-cream mixture from Step 1 and stir to incorporate.
3. Pour sugar-egg mixture into remaining cream in saucepan and stir. Pour into four 6 oz. ramekins and place into a baking dish.
4. Fill dish with boiling water halfway up the sides of the ramekins. Bake at 325°F for 30-40 minutes, until centers are just set.
5. Remove from grill and sprinkle a thin layer of sugar on top of each custard.
6. Tip: Use a butane torch to gradually melt sugar until caramelized and golden brown on top.

Low Carb Blueberry Cobbler

Cooking Time: 45 Min

Ingredients:

- Fresh or Frozen Blueberries - 2 Cups
- Water - 1/4 Cup
- Lemon Juice - 1 Tablespoon
- Monkfruit Sweetener - 2 Tablespoons
- Stevia - 10 Drops
- Xanthan Gum - 1/8 Teaspoon
- Softened Butter Chopped into Pieces - 1/4 Cup
- Coconut Flour - 1/3 Cup
- Additional Monkfruit Sweetener - 1/3 Cup
- Ground Cinnamon - 1 Tablespoon

Directions:

1. In sauce pan add blueberries, water, lemon juice & sweetener. Bring to a light boil and add xanthan gum. Stir occasionally as it thickens. Then remove from heat.
2. For crumble topping, mix coconut flour, monkfruit & cinnamon. Combine well, then add butter. Mix with fingers until well incorporated & crumbly.
3. Pour blueberry sauce into cast iron skillet & top with cinnamon crumb topping. Bake on grill heated to 350° for about 30 mins or until it bubbles & topping browns.

Spooky Brain Cinnamon Buns

Cooking Time: 30 Min

Ingredients:

- One Can Cinnamon Rolls
- Strawberry Jam
- Cinnamon Roll Frosting

Directions:

1. Layer the dough in a pan up against each other in and shaped it to look like a brain.
2. Heat oven or grill to 350°
3. Bake the cinnamon rolls for 30 minutes
4. While the cinnamon buns are baking, add the strawberry fruit spread to the icing and mixed it.
5. Then add the icing on to the cinnamon buns when they are done baking.

Strawberry And Rhubarb Crumble Pie

Cooking Time: 35-40 Min

Ingredients:

- 1¼ C. and ¾ C. all-purpose flour, plus 2 Tbsp. for filling
- 1 C. unsalted butter, diced and divided
- 1 C. sugar
- ½ C. light brown sugar
- 1 large egg
- 2 C. fresh rhubarb, cut into ½" dice
- 2 C. fresh strawberries, stemmed and sliced
- ¼ Tsp. orange zest, finely grated, optional
- 2 Tbsp. cold water, or more as needed
- 1 Tsp. vanilla extract
- Cold water, as needed

Directions:

1. Add 1¼ C. flour and salt to a large bowl and cut in ½ C. of butter with a pastry blender until the mixture resembles coarse crumbs. 2. Gradually add cold water to crumb mixture, until dough holds together when pressed. 3. Shape into a ball and wrap in plastic. Refrigerate 30 minutes. 4. Turn dough onto a floured surface and roll into a circle large enough to cover a buttered pie dish. Place dough into pie dish, trim the edges and prick the bottom with a fork.
2. Crumble Topping
3. In a medium bowl, combine ¾ C. flour, light brown sugar, and remaining ½ C. of butter Mix using a pastry blender or electric mixer until it resembles coarse crumbs.
4. Filling:Pre-heat grill to 400°F. In a large bowl, whisk 2 Tbsp. flour, egg, 1 C. sugar and vanilla together, until sugar is dissolved. 2. Add strawberries and rhubarb and mix until just blended. Let stand for 30 minutes at room temperature. 3. After 30 minutes, pour filling into pie crust. Sprinkle crumble topping evenly over pie and cover loosely with foil. Bake at 400°F for 35-40 minutes or until filling is bubbly and crumble topping is golden brown. Remove foil during the last 10 minutes.
5. Cool on wire rack before slicing and serving.

Pineapple Upside-down Cake

Cooking Time: 45 Min

Ingredients:

- 20 oz. can pineapple slices in juice, drained, with juice reserved
- 6 oz. jar maraschino cherries without stems, drained
- 1 box yellow cake mix
- ¼ C. unsalted butter
- 1 C. brown sugar
- Vegetable oil, according to box directions
- Eggs, according to box directions

Directions:

1. Pre-heat grill to 350°F. Melt butter in a cast iron pan and sprinkle brown sugar evenly over butter.
2. Place pineapple slices in pan on top of brown sugar and place a cherry in the center of each pineapple slice. Add remaining cherries around slices.
3. Add enough water to reserved pineapple juice to measure 1 C. Make cake batter according to package directions, substituting pineapple juice mixture for water. Slowly pour batter over pineapple and cherries in an even layer.
4. Bake at 350°F for 45 minutes or until a toothpick inserted into the center comes out clean. Run a knife around the side of the pan to loosen cake. Place a serving plate upside down onto the pan and turn plate and pan over.
5. Allow topping to drizzle over cake, then remove pan and allow cake to cool before slicing. Store covered in refrigerator.

Akorn Cinnamon Streusel Coffee Cake

Cooking Time: 2 Hrs

Ingredients:

- 1 ½ cups all-purpose flour (Topping)
- 1 ¼ cups packed light-brown sugar (Topping)
- 1 ½ tsp ground cinnamon (Topping)
- 1 ½ sticks cold salted butter, cut into fifths (Topping)
- 1 ½ cups chopped toasted pecans (Topping)
- 1 tsp kosher salt (Topping)
- 1 ¼ tsp baking powder (Cake)
- ½ tsp baking soda (Cake)
- 1 stick salted butter (room temperature) (Cake)
- 2 cups all-purpose flour (Cake)
- 1 ¼ cup granulated sugar (Cake)
- ½ tsp kosher salt (Cake)
- 2 large eggs (Cake)
- 1 ½ tsp vanilla extract (Cake)
- 1 cup plain greek yogurt (Cake)
- 1 cup powdered sugar (Glaze)
- 2 tbsp milk (Cake)

Directions:

1. Oktoberfest doesn't have to be just brats and sauerkraut. Bryan Head, @thebbqhead, made a classic Cinnamon Streusel Coffee Cake recipe and used his AKORN to bake it!
2. Toast pecans. Preheat oven to 275°F. In a bowl, melt a half stick of salted butter and toss pecans in the butter. Lay out pecans evenly on a baking sheet and toast for one hour flipping every 15 minutes. Let cool. Chop coarsely and set aside. Make the streusel topping. Mix together flour, ¾ cup brown sugar, 1 tsp cinnamon, and 1 tsp of salt. Cut in butter with sturdy fork or rub in with your fingers until pea-sized clumps remain. Mix in ½ cup chopped pecans. Refrigerate until ready to use. Make the streusel center. Mix together remaining ½ cup brown sugar, ½ tsp cinnamon, and 1 cup pecans. Prepare AKORN for indirect heat at 325°F. Make your cake: Butter the pan. Use a 9-inch tube pan with a removable bottom for best results. Sift in flour, baking powder, baking soda, and ½ tsp salt into a mixing bowl. Beat butter and granulated sugar with a mixer on medium speed for 2 minutes. Beat in eggs, one at a time, then vanilla. Beat in flour mixture in 3 stages alternating with greek yogurt, beginning and ending with the flour. Continue to beat at medium speed until well combined. Add half the batter into the pan. Sprinkle on the streusel

center mixture evenly. Add the rest of the batter and spread evenly using a spatula. Sprinkle on the streusel topping evenly over batter. Bake until cake shows golden brown and a toothpick inserted into the center comes out clean, about 1 hour. Transfer pan to a wire rack to cool. Remove cake from pan. Make the glaze: Mix together powdered sugar and milk until you get your desired consistency. Drizzle over cake and down the sides and middle. Slice and enjoy!

Cheesecake Stuffed Apples

Cooking Time: 60 Min

Ingredients:

- Medium Baking Apples (I used Pink Lady) - 4
- Softened Cream Cheese - 8 Ounces
- Egg - 1
- Sugar - 1/3 Cup
- Cinnamon - 1/4 Teaspoon
- Crushed Graham Crackers - 1/4 Cup
- Prepared Caramel Sauce for Garnish

Directions:

1. Light AKORN and heat to 325
2. Cut bottoms of apples just enough to make them stand up straight
3. Hollow out apples with an apple corer or melon baller. Leave a ¼ inch of flesh around sides and bottom
4. Mix cream cheese, egg, sugar, vanilla, and cinnamon together until smooth
5. Spoon cream cheese mixture into each apple, leaving 1/2 inch space at the top
6. Sprinkle tops with graham crackers
7. Place apples in a small aluminum pan and place on grill
8. Allow to bake for 50-60 minutes. Filling should look semi set and apples should be soft
9. Allow to cool at room temperature then place in refrigerator until cold
10. Before serving, drizzle with caramel sauce

Smoked Chocolate Chip Cookies

Cooking Time: 15 To 20 Min

Ingredients:

- 2.25 Cups All Purpose Flour
- 2 Sticks of Butter
- 1 tsp Salt
- 1/2 Cup Sugar
- 1 Cup Light Brown Sugar
- 3 tsp Baking Powder
- 2 Eggs
- 1 tsp Vanilla Extract
- 2 Tbsp Milk
- Chocolate Chips (Your Choice with How Much)
- Chopped Pecans (Your Choice How Much)

Directions:

1. Melt the butter in a small pan.
2. Sift the flour, salt, & baking powder into a bowl.
3. Pour the butter in a mixing bowl & cream with the white & brown sugars.
4. Add the eggs, milk, and vanilla to the creamed sugar & mix.
5. Slowly add the flour mixture to the wet ingredients, beating constantly.
6. Mix in the chocolate chips & pecans.
7. Place the cookie dough in the fridge for a minimum of 30 minutes.
8. Heat your Char-griller Smoker/Grill to 350° or you can bake them in an oven at the same temperature.

9. Using a spoon make the cookies into a ball shape and place on pizza stone or cookie sheet using parchment paper or peach butcher paper.
10. Place in smoker/grill and smoke for 15-20 minutes or until golden brown.
11. Remove the cookies from the smoker/grill and allow them to cool for 10 minutes.
12. Enjoy.

Puffy Pancake With Fruit Compote

Cooking Time: 15 Min

Ingredients:

- 4 large eggs
- 1 C. all-purpose flour
- 1 C. milk
- 2 Tbsp. granulated sugar
- ¼ Tsp. salt
- 2 Tbsp. butter
- 2 ripe bananas, peeled and sliced
- 1 pint blueberries
- 1 Tbsp. granulated sugar
- 1 Tbsp. lemon juice
- Confectioners' sugar

Directions:

1. Pre-heat grill to 425°F, place a 10" cast iron skillet on grill and heat until very hot.
2. In a blender at medium speed, blend eggs, milk, flour, sugar, and salt together until smooth.
3. Remove skillet from the grill, add butter and swirl until melted. Pour batter into hot skillet and bake for 15 minutes until puffy and golden brown on the edges.
4. In a large bowl, toss bananas and blueberries with sugar and lemon juice to make compote.
5. Spoon compote onto pancake and sprinkle with confectioner's sugar. To serve, cut into wedges.

Lou's Peach Cobbler

Cooking Time: 50 Min

Ingredients:

- 5 large peaches, peeled, pitted and sliced
- 1 C. and 3 Tbsp. all-purpose flour
- ¼ C. brown sugar
- 1 C. sugar
- 1 Tsp. baking powder
- 1 Tsp. lemon juice
- ½ Tsp. grated lemon peel
- ½ Tsp. ground cinnamon
- ¼ Tsp. salt
- ¼ Tsp. ground nutmeg
- 1 large egg, lightly beaten
- ½ C. butter, melted

Directions:

1. Pre-heat grill to 375°F. Combine brown sugar, 3 Tbsp. flour, lemon juice, grated lemon peel and cinnamon in a bowl and mix well. 2. Place sliced peaches in a large cast iron pot with a lid and sprinkle sugar mixture over top. Do not stir. 3. Transfer to grill and allow to cook at 375°F for 10 minutes. 4. While peaches are cooking, make the dough. Add 1 C. flour, sugar, baking powder, salt, nutmeg, egg and melted butter to a food processor, pulse to combine and mix well until a dough forms. 5. Remove peaches from grill, tear dough into medium to large pieces and place over top of peaches until covered. Replace lid and return to grill. 6. Bake at 375°F for 40 minutes.
2. To serve, scoop onto a plate and top with whipped cream or vanilla ice cream. Enjoy!

Deep Dish Apple Pie

Cooking Time: 40 Min

Ingredients:

- 8 medium tart apples, cored, peeled and sliced (makes 10 C.)
- 2 C. and 3 Tbsp. all-purpose flour
- ½ C. shortening
- 2 large eggs
- ¼ C. cold water
- 2 Tbsp. apple cider vinegar
- 1 Tsp. lemon juice
- ¼ C. sugar
- ¼ C. brown sugar
- 1 Tsp. ground cinnamon
- ½ Tsp. ground nutmeg
- 1 Tbsp. milk
- Unsalted butter, softened

Directions:

1. Pre-heat grill to 350°. Add 2 C. flour to a large bowl and cut in shortening. Mix until crumbly.
2. In a small bowl, whisk 1 egg, water and apple cider vinegar together and gradually add to crumb mixture, tossing with a fork until dough holds together when pressed.
3. Shape into a ball and wrap in plastic. Refrigerate 30 minutes or overnight, if desired.
4. Filling: In a large bowl, toss apples with lemon juice, sugars, remaining flour, cinnamon and nutmeg until evenly coated. Arrange in a single layer on a baking sheet. 2. Place pan onto grill and bake at 350°F with lid closed for 10-15 minutes, until apples release their juices. 3. While apples are baking, turn dough out onto a floured surface and roll into 2 circles large enough to cover a buttered pie dish with an overhang of at least 1". Place 1 dough into pie dish and prick the bottom with a fork. 5. Remove apples from grill and place evenly into prepared pie dish. Place the other pie dough on top of the apples and crimp the edges. 6. In a small bowl, whisk 1 egg together with milk to make egg wash and brush over pie. Cut slits in top. 7. Bake at 350°F for 40 minutes or until crust is golden brown. Remove from grill and run a knife around the side of the pan to loosen pie.
5. Cool on a wire rack and serve with ice cream, if desired. Enjoy!

Chocolate Lava Cake

Cooking Time: 15 Min

Ingredients:

- ½ C. all-purpose flour
- 1 stick unsalted butter
- 2 oz. bittersweet chocolate
- 2 oz. semisweet chocolate
- 1¼ C. powdered sugar
- 2 eggs and 3 egg yolks
- 1 Tsp. vanilla extract

Directions:

1. Pre-heat grill to 425°F. Spray four 6 oz. ramekins with baking spray and place on a baking sheet.
2. Melt the butter, bittersweet chocolate and semisweet chocolate together in a pan on medium heat, stirring constantly. Stir in the sugar until dissolved.
3. Whisk in the eggs and egg yolks, then add vanilla. Gradually stir in flour. Divide the mixture among the ramekins.
4. Bake until the sides are firm and the centers are soft, about 15 minutes. Let stand 1 minute.
5. To serve, plate each cake while warm and serve with vanilla ice cream.

Skillet Brownie On The Grill

Ingredients:

- Softened Butter- 2 Tablespoons
- Heavy Whipping Cream- 1 Tablespoon
- Large Egg- 1
- Erythritol Blend (or Sweeter of Your Choice)- 3 Tablespoons
- Cocoa Powder- 2.5 Tablespoons
- Almond Flour- 2.5 Tablespoons
- Pinch of Sea Salt

Directions:

1. Preheat the grill to 350°.
2. Mix together all of the ingredients until smooth and spread the batter in a greased mini cast iron skillet.
3. Place the skillet directly on the preheated grill grate, close the grill, and bake for 6 to 8 minutes—or just until set. Do not over bake in the grill, as the hot skillet will continue to bake the brownie as it sits.
4. Top with sugar free vanilla ice cream, sugar free chocolate syrup, and a sliced strawberry. Serve warm.
5. This serves one to two, but can be doubled or tripled for more servings. Bake each batch in its own mini skillet.

Smoked Apple Crumb Pie

Cooking Time: 75 Min

Ingredients:

- Frozen Pie Crust
- 1 Cup Flour
- 1/3 Cup White Sugar
- Lemon Juice - 1/2 Tbs
- Lemon Zest - 1/3 tsp
- Cinnamon - 1 tsp
- Nutmeg - 1/8 tsp
- Flour - 3 Tbs (Topping)
- 1/3 Cup White Sugar
- 1/2 Cup Packed Brown Sugar
- 1/2 Cup Oats
- Stick of Butter

Directions:

1. Add Smokin' Stone to AKORN, add chunks of Applewood, and preheat grill to 350 degrees.
2. Combine flour, sugar, brown sugar, oats and butter. Mix with fork to make topping.
3. Peel, core and slice apples into thin slices.
4. Toss apples with sugar, lemon juice and zest, cinnamon, nutmeg, and flour.
5. Layer apples in pie shell and pour juice over apples.
6. Put crumb topping on top of apples.
7. Bake for 1 hour and 15 minutes.
8. Serve warm with ice cream or whipped cream.

Smoked White Chocolate Christmas Candy

Cooking Time: 1 Hrs

Ingredients:

- 3 Cups Cheerios
- 3 Cups Corn Chex
- 3 Cups Peanut Butter Chex
- 1 Cup Butter Snaps Pretzels
- 1.5 Cups M&Ms
- 32 oz white Chocolate Chips

Directions:

1. Smoke white chocolate chips using your Char-Griller Offset charcoal smoker.
2. Add 6 lit charcoals to the far side of firebox along with a mild smoking wood chunk. Maple

wood goes well with this recipe. Feel free to leave vents fully open.

3. You will need 2 foil baking pans. Fill pan number one with a layer of ice cubes. About ¼ of the way full. Add white chocolate chips to the second pan. Place pan with white chocolate on top of the pan with the ice.
4. Place stacked pans in cooking chamber of your smoker. Keep as far away from fire box side as possible.
5. Smoke for 30-45 minutes. For a milder smoke flavor try 30 minutes. To impart a stronger smoke flavor, try 45 minutes.
6. Melt white chocolate over heat source.
7. Add white chocolate to a large saucepan or keep in foil pan.
8. Over medium heat or lit coals, melt until white chocolate is a smooth consistency able to be drizzled. Be sure to stir often and do not over melt.
9. In a large mixing bowl or 2 foil pans, combine dry ingredients (cheerios, corn chex, peanut butter chex, pretzels, and m&m's) making sure to evenly distribute the ingredients.
10. Drizzle white chocolate on the dry mixture. Stir in making sure to coat all the mixture in the white chocolate.
11. Lay out on parchment paper or leave in foil pans as a nice thin layer to dry/cool for 1 hour.
12. Break into small to medium pieces and enjoy!
13. This stores well in the fridge and the freezer!

Smoked Blueberry Crisp

Cooking Time: 45 Min

Ingredients:

- Blueberries - 5 Cups
- Sugar - 2 Tablespoons
- Ground Ginger - 1/2 Teaspoon
- Brown Sugar - 1/2 Cup
- Flour - 1/2 Cup
- Rolled Oats - 3/4 Cup
- Cinnamon - 1 Tablespoon
- Melted Butter - 1/2 Cup

Directions:

1. To begin, put your blueberries into a half size foil pan and spread them out evenly.
2. Mix your sugar and ground ginger and evenly coat all the blueberries.
3. Mix the remaining ingredients together and distribute evenly over the top of the blueberries.
4. Bring your AKORN Kamado up to 375 degrees with a chunk of cherry wood for smoke and the Smokin' Stone in place to set up for indirect cooking.
5. Once the smoke is a clean smoke, that is thin and blue, place your half steamer pan on the AKORN for forty minutes. After forty minutes remove from AKORN, let cool and enjoy.

Faux Apple Pie

Ingredients:

- 3 Cups Almond Flour (Crust)
- Baking Powder - 3 Tbsp (Crust)
- 1/3 Cup Xanthan Gum (Crust)
- 1/2 Cup and 1 Tbsp Coconut Flour (Crust)
- Apple Cider Vinegar - 2 Tbsp
- 3 Eggs, Whisked (Crust)
- Water - 3 Tbsp (Crust)
- 6 Chayote Squash, peeled, cored, sliced thin (Filling)
- 1 Cup Lakanto Golden Sweetener (Filling)
- Cinnamon - 2 Tbsp (Filling)
- Nutmeg - 1 tsp (Filling)
- Vanilla - 2 Tbsp (Filling)

- Lemon Juice - 3 Tbsp (Filling)
- 1/4 Cup Lankanto Classic Granulated Sweetener (Filling)
- Butter - 3 Tbsp (Filling)
- 1 Bag Cinnamon Pecan Lollis Cookie Clusters (Topping)

Directions:

1. Mix all wet ingredients in one bowl, set aside.
2. Mix all dry ingredients in large bowl, once dry ingredients are combined, slowly add were ingredients.
3. Mix with a spoon as good as you can, then knead with hands.
4. Shape into a ball, wrap in saran wrap and refrigerate for 2 hours.
5. Combine in a sauce pan, cook over medium heat for 20 minutes.
6. Add more sweetener if desired.
7. Remove from heat to cool.
8. Roll out dough between 2 sheets of parchment paper until 1/4 inch thin, place in aluminum pie pan - trim edges.
9. Poke holes in crust with fork.
10. Preheat grill to 325-350°.
11. Place pie crust on grill over indirect heat.
12. Cook about 5-8 minutes until crust starts to turn golden.
13. Remove from grill, add pie filling and even spread the crumbled Lollis Cookie Clusters over the top until filling is covered.
14. Place pie back on grill over indirect heat for about 25-30 minutes until nicely browned.
15. Let pie cool completely before serving.
16. Pairs well with vanilla Rebel Creamery ice cream.

Guinness Cupcakes With Whiskey Salted Caramel Buttercream

Cooking Time: 25 Min

Ingredients:

- 1 Devils food Cake Mix
- 1 3.9 Oz Instant Chocolate Pudding
- 1 Cup Sour Cream
- 1/2 Cup Guinness
- 1/2 Cup of Oil
- 4 Eggs
- 3/4 Cup Mini Chocolate Chips
- 1 Cup of Light Brown Sugar
- 1/4 Cup of Butter
- 1/4 Cup of Milk
- 1/4 Cup of Whiskey
- 1/4 Tbsp Sea Salt
- 4 Sticks of Unsalted Butter
- 6 Cup of Powdered Sugar
- 1/4 Cup of Salted Caramel

Directions:

1. Heat Akorn to 325 for indirect heat and add liners to a cupcake pan Add cake mix, pudding, sour cream, oil, Guinness, eggs, and ½ c. of the chocolate chips in a large bowl and mix together until combined Divide batter evenly into 24 cupcakes Bake for 20 minutes or until middle of the cake springs back when gently pushed down or until a toothpick inserted into the center comes out clean While cupcakes are cooling, add brown sugar, 1/4 c. butter, milk, and sea salt to a medium sauce pan On medium heat, melt caramel mixture stirring frequently until mixture starts to simmer Allow to simmer without stirring for 5-7 minutes until thickened. Remove from heat and allow to cool To make the frosting, add

butter to mixer and beat until smooth and creamy. Slowly add the powdered sugar and beat until light and fluffy. Add caramel to frosting and beat until combined Top cooled cupcakes with a spoonful of buttercream and spread across the cupcake I like to add a drizzle of the leftover caramel on top of the frosted cupcakes with a little sprinkle of the leftover chocolate chips

2. If caramel starts to thicken too much to drizzle, you can microwave it for 10 seconds

PORK

Smoked Pork Loin

Cooking Time: 2 Hrs

Ingredients:

- Pork Loin
- 2 Tbsp Of Your Favorite Rub Of Any Kind

Directions:

1. Remove loin from packaging and remove any silverskin if necessary. Cover the loin in the 2 Tbsp of rub Bring your cooker up to 300 degrees, set it up for indirect cooking and add 1 small piece of hickory wood. Place the pork loin on the grate and place a leave in thermometer in it and set it for 4 degrees. Once the loin hits 145 degrees internal temperature remove it from the cooker, cut it into 1 inch chops and serve

Grilled Stuffed Pork Chops

Cooking Time: 15 Min

Ingredients:

- 1" thick bone-in pork chops
- 1 Tbsp. unsalted butter
- 2 Tbsp. chopped almonds
- 4 C. baby spinach, finely chopped
- 4 oz. cream cheese
- ¼ Tsp. cayenne pepper
- ¼ Tsp. salt
- Original All-Purpose BBQ Rub, to taste

Directions:

1. Pre-heat grill to 375°F. Rinse the pork chops and pat dry with paper towel. Cut a deep pocket in the side of each chop with a small sharp knife, cutting toward the bone but not all the way through. 2. In a medium bowl, combine butter, chopped almonds, baby spinach, cream cheese, cayenne pepper and salt and mix well to make stuffing. 3. Transfer mixture to a piping bag without a tip, fill pork chops with mixture and secure with toothpicks. 4. Generously season both sides of each chop with Original All-Purpose BBQ rub, or your favorite rub, to taste. 5. Place stuffed pork chops on the grill over direct heat at 375°F for 6 minutes per side, turning halfway through for good sear marks. Move to indirect side of grill to finish cooking if needed.
2. Pork chops are done when internal temperature reaches 145°F. Remove from grill and set aside to rest for 5 minutes and remove toothpicks before serving. Enjoy!

Simple Smoked Bbq Pork Belly

Cooking Time: 2.5 Hrs

Ingredients:

- Redmond's Pink Himalayan Salt- 1 Teaspoon
- Redmond's Organic Garlic Pepper- 1 Teaspoon
- Butter- 1 stick
- G Hughes Sweet & Spicy BBQ Sauce-1/4-1/2 Cup

Directions:

1. Pat pork belly dry with paper towel
2. Season to taste with Pink salt & garlic pepper
3. Baste with bbq sauce
4. Smoke at 250° in aluminum pan with butter for 2.5 hours. Then place directly over the coals for 5 minutes
5. Add more BBQ glaze if desired.

St. Louis-style Ribs

Cooking Time: 5 Hrs

Ingredients:

- 3 racks of ribs
- Ribs BBQ rub, to taste
- 1 can Coca-Cola
- 1 C. molasses
- ½ C. agave nectar
- ½ C. Jack Daniels Tennessee whiskey (or a good bourbon whiskey)
- ½ C. apple cider vinegar
- ¼ C. honey, and more as needed for wrapping ribs
- 1 Tbsp. cayenne pepper
- Apple juice
- Brown sugar
- 12 oz. bottle of squeeze butter

Directions:

1. Rinse rib racks and pat dry with paper towel. Remove membrane from each rack by carefully prying back using the back of a sharp knife. Discard membrane. Flip racks and trim loose ends and excess fat.Tip: Use a paper towel to help hold the membrane, as it's slippery.
2. Season ribs generously with Ribs BBQ Rub, or your favorite rub.
3. When setting up the grill, use a full chimney of unlit charcoal in the attached Side Fire Box and pour another ½ chimney of hot coals on top to ensure good smoke and a temperature of 275°F. Add Applewood chunks on top.
4. Adjust the charcoal grate to the highest setting in the main compartment. Place an aluminum pan on the grate and fill halfway with apple juice. Smoke ribs for 1 hour and mist with apple juice. Close lid and smoke for another 3 hours. 5. After 3 hours, remove ribs from grill and wrap. Before wrapping, spread a layer of brown sugar, butter and honey onto aluminum foil. Place ribs meat side down and wrap securely. 6. Transfer wrapped ribs to the grill and smoke at 275°F for another hour. 7. During the last 10-20 minutes of smoking the ribs, make the glaze. Combine 1 can of Coca-Cola, molasses, agave nectar, whiskey, apple cider vinegar, honey and cayenne pepper in a saucepan and bring to a boil, stirring occasionally. Reduce heat to a simmer until glaze is thickened.
5. Remove ribs from the grill and carefully drain juices before brushing with glaze, slicing and serving.

Flat Iron Griddle Breakfast Sandwich

Cooking Time: 5 Min

Ingredients:

- 2 Cups Of Kodiak Cakes Pancake And Waffle Mix
- 2 Cups Of Water
- 6 Eggs
- Egg Rings
- Syrup
- 1 Pack Of Bacon

Directions:

1. Mix pancake and waffle mix with water until the mix is no longer lumpy. Place egg rings on griddle and pour pancake batter into the egg rings , add a little swirl of syrup while batter is cooking. Once the batter has a nice bubble to it remove the egg ring and flip the griddle cake. Scramble or fry your eggs and cook the bacon , construct sandwich and enjoy

Ultimate Pork Belly Sliders

Cooking Time: 2:15 Hrs

Ingredients:

- 4 lb. pork belly
- Yellow mustard
- Original All-Purpose BBQ rub, to taste
- Your favorite sweet BBQ rub, to taste
- Hawaiian sweet rolls or your favorite roll for sliders
- Your favorite toppings
- Your favorite BBQ sauce

Directions:

1. Remove the skin from the pork belly and season the top generously with a layer of yellow mustard, followed by Original All-Purpose BBQ rub and your favorite sweet BBQ sauce, to taste.
2. Pre-heat grill to 275°F for indirect heat with a Smokin' Stone. Allow the belly to smoke for 2 hours or until internal temperature reaches 175°F. Remove the belly from the grill and allow to rest.
3. After removing the pork belly and Smokin' Stone, stir the charcoal and open up both vents to allow the grill to reach maximum temperature for searing.
4. While the grill is heating up, slice the pork belly into ¼" thick strips and arrange on the grill. Work in batches if needed. Fry the belly for 3 minutes on each side, to allow the fat to render. Season the belly with BBQ rub again, if desired.
5. Slice the pack of Hawaiian sweet rolls in half and arrange the pork belly on the bottom half. Cover with the top half and brush with melted butter and garlic, if desired. Place the rolls in a large pan and back onto the grill to crisp up for 10 minutes.
6. Remove the pan from the grill and allow the rolls to cool slightly before slicing into individual sliders. Add your favorite toppings and sauce and enjoy!

Grilled Pork Chops

Ingredients:

- 4 Bone-In or Boneless Pork Chops
- 1/4 Cup of Olive Oil
- 2 Tbsp of Soy Sauce
- 1 Tbsp of Worcestershire Sauce
- 1 Tsp of Crushed Red Pepper Flakes
- 1/2 Tsp of Cumin
- 1 Tbsp of Honey
- 1 Tsp of Chopped Parsley
- Kosher Salt
- Ground Black Pepper

Directions:

1. In a bowl, mix the olive oil, soy sauce, Worcestershire sauce, red pepper flakes, cumin, honey and desired amount of salt and pepper. Add the marinade and pork chops to a resealable bag and allow to marinate for 1 hour up to overnight. Heat the grill to medium heat and place each pork chop on the grill, cooking for 6-8 minutes per side or until the internal temperature of the thickest part reaches 145°F. Remove the chops from the grill and allow them to rest for 5-10 minutes before garnishing with parsley and serving with desired sides. Enjoy!

Smoked Chili Hotdogs

Cooking Time: 20-30 Min

Ingredients:

- 8 hotdogs
- 8 hotdog buns
- 8 slices of cheese

- 1 cup of shredded cheese
- 1 can chili sauce
- 4 Tbsp. butter
- 1/2 Tsp. granulated garlic

Directions:

1. Place hotdog buns (whole) in a greased 9x13 pan
2. Cut hotdog sized slots with a knife
3. With finger, pack cut part of bun down
4. Melt butter and garlic
5. Baste buns with the butter and garlic mixture
6. Place a slice of cheese into each bun
7. Add some chili
8. Place the hotdog on top of the chili
9. Add more chili
10. Top with shredded cheese
11. Sprinkle with parsley flakes
12. Place on smoker at 250°F
13. Smoke for 20-30 minutes or until cheese is melted

Grilled Pork And Sweet Potato Verde Chili

Cooking Time: 3.5 Hrs

Ingredients:

- 2 Lbs Pork
- 2 Large Sweet Potatoes - Diced
- 3 Ears of Corn on the Cob
- 1 Bunch Cilantro - Stems Cut from Leaves and Set Aside
- 2 Cloves of Garlic
- 3 Tbsp Ground Cumin
- 1/2 Cup olive Oil or Avocado Oil
- 2 Cups Salsa Verde
- 6 Cups Chicken Stock
- 1 Can White Beans
- Salt and Pepper to taste
- Garnish: Cilantro, Radish, Red Onion, and/or Sour Cream

Directions:

1. Remove stems from fresh cilantro, and add to blender with garlic cloves, oil, cumin, and a pinch of s&p. Pulse until smooth and combined.
2. Preheat Char-Griller to high heat, I recommend charcoal for this recipe as it will add even more flavor.
3. In a large bowl, transfer corn, pork, and sweet potato pieces. Pour blended marinade over the ingredients and toss to combine. Once grill is heated, add all to grill, and cook until charred on each side, 6-8 mins per side. Remove and set aside.
4. Once the grilled items are cool to the touch, dice sweet potatoes and pork into similar sized pieces, and cut corn off the cob. Transfer these items to a soup pot, adding salsa verde, & chicken stock. Bring to a simmer over low.
5. Add ½ cup chopped cilantro leaves, the white beans, and S&P to taste. Simmer on low partially covered for 3 hours, until pork is fall apart tender, and chili has thickened. Serve with garnishes of choice and enjoy! Leftover Chili can stay in the fridge for up to 7 days, and frozen for 6 months.

Smoked Meatballs With Sweet And Sour Sauce

Cooking Time: 30 Min

Ingredients:

- 3/4 Cup Panko Breadcrumbs (Meatballs)
- 1/2 Yellow Onion, Minced (Meatballs)
- 1/2 Pounds 80/20 Ground Beef (Meatballs)
- 1 Egg (Meatballs)
- 2 Garlic Cloves, Minced (Meatballs)
- 1.5 tsp Worcestershire Sauce (Meatballs)

- 1 Tbsp Bacon Fat (Melted, Cooled) (Meatballs)
- 1/2 tsp Kosher Salt (Meatballs)
- 3/4 tsp Black Pepper
- 1 Tbsp Cornstarch (Sauce)
- 1/4 Cup Water (Sauce)
- 1/4 Cup Apple Cider Vinegar (Sauce)
- 1/2 Cup Brown Sugar (Sauce)
- 1/4 Cup Ketchup (Sauce)
- 1 Tbsp Soy Sauce (Sauce)

Directions:

1. Prepare smoker grill for 375°F add mild smoking wood for smoke flavor.
2. In a large mixing bowl, add ground beef, ground pork, melted bacon fat, onion, and breadcrumbs. Mix together with hands to coat. Let sit for a few minutes.
3. Add remaining meatball ingredients and mix with hands to combine.
4. Scoop out level tablespoons of the meat mixture and set on work surface. Roll each in hands to form a smooth meatball.
5. Spray down a racked baking tray with oil. Place meatballs on rack.
6. Bake/smoke for 30 minutes or until browned. Cook to at least 165°F internal temperature. Remove from heat and transfer meatballs to a large bowl immediately to avoid sticking.
7. Combine all ingredients in a small saucepan over medium heat. Whisk to combine.
8. Bring to simmer, stirring frequently. Then simmer until sauce thickens like maple syrup. (3-5 minutes)
9. Cover meatballs with sweet and sour sauce sauce. Transfer to a serving dish with toothpicks and remaining dipping sauce.
10. Keep warm and stir occasionally prior to serving.
11. Enjoy!

Flavor Pro Smoked Pork Shoulder

Cooking Time: 90 Minutes Per Pound And Then 1 Hour Rest Hrs

Ingredients:

- 5 to 6 Pound Bone-In Pork Shoulder or Boston Butt
- Char-Griller Rib Rub
- Spray Bottle Full of Apple Juice and Oil

Directions:

1. Trim excess fat from the pork shoulder. (Skip this step if it is Boston Butt.) Score the remaining fat with a sharp knife.
2. Rub a liberal amount of Rib Spice Rub on the pork. Make sure each side is evenly coated.
3. Place pork in the fridge for at least 12 hours.
4. Remove pork from fridge one hour before placing on the grill.
5. Cover the left-most and center Wood Product Zones of the Flavor Drawer with foil to catch the grease.
6. Place 15 to 20 charcoal briquettes in the far right side of the Flavor Drawer.
7. Turn the burners on high and ignite. Allow the briquettes to fully ash over.
8. Once the briquettes have ashed over, add two to three wood chunks to the charcoal.
9. To Use a Log: Place a log of no more than 3 inches in diameter and 7 inches long the right-most wood product zone. Light using the right most burner.
10. The log should take about 5 to 6 minutes to ignite.

11. After the log has ignited, turn off the gas burner and allow the grill to preheat.
12. Using a Grilling Glove, adjust the smokestacks until the internal temperature of the pit holds steady at 225.
13. Place the pork over the foil and close the grill.
14. Baste pork with Apple juice every 30 to 60 minutes.
15. Make sure to keep an eye on the pit temperature. Add another log every hour or so.
16. Smoke until internal temperature is 195 to 210 degrees Fahrenheit and remove from grill.
17. Tip: If your pork shoulder hits the dreaded "stall" (won't get above 165 degrees Fahrenheit or starts dropping, wrap it in foil, add some apple juice and place back on the grill. This will get it going again.
18. Allow pork to rest for 30 minutes to an hour for best results.

Pork Tenderloin Sliders

Cooking Time: 8-10 Min

Ingredients:

- (2) 1 lb. pork tenderloins
- Salt and pepper, to taste
- Olive oil, for brushing
- Slider buns

Directions:

1. Pre-heat grill to 400°F. Rinse tenderloins and pat dry with paper towel. 2. Generously season with salt and pepper or use Original All-Purpose BBQ rub, to taste. 3. Place pork tenderloins on the grill at 400°F for 4 minutes per side, brushing with olive oil occasionally, and turning to ensure good sear marks on each side. Pork is done when internal temperature reaches 140°F. 4. Toast slider buns for 1-2 minutes before serving.
2. Brush with a layer of BBQ sauce and allow pork to rest for 10 minutes before slicing and serving on toasted slider buns.

Flavor Pro Quick And Easy Grilled Pork Tenderloin

Ingredients:

- 2 Pork Tenderloin
- 2 tsp Paprika
- 1 tsp Garlic Powder
- 1 tsp Cilantro
- 1 tsp Oregano
- Salt and Pepper to Taste
- Olive Oil

Directions:

1. Blend spices together in a bowl. Rub pork with olive oil and then season liberally on both sides with spice blend.
2. Set up the Flavor Pro for direct cooking. Ignite burners and turn to medium high.
3. Place pork on the grill and cook for 8 to 10 minutes per side or until the internal temperature reads 165 degrees.
4. Remove from grill and let rest for 10 minutes.

Gravity 980 Smoked Pork Shoulder

Cooking Time: 3-4 Hrs

Ingredients:

- 1 7-9 Lb. Pork Shoulder, trimmed
- 3 Tbsp of Yellow Mustard
- 2 Tbsp Kosher Salt
- 2 Tbsp Black Pepper
- 2 Tbsp Garlic Powder
- 2 Tbsp Onion Powder
- 1 Tbsp Paprika

- 1 Tbsp Cumin
- 1 Cup of Apple Juice or Apple Cider Vinegar
- 1/2 Cup of Water

Directions:

1. No more babysitting your pork shoulder with the Gravity 980. Easily prepare an awesome pork shoulder for stellar dishes like sandwiches, mac and cheese or even nachos.
2. In a small bowl, combine seasonings, and in a spray, bottle combine apple cider/juice and water. Thoroughly rub mustard all over the surface of your pork shoulder then coat with all the seasonings. Remove the fire shutter from your Gravity 980 then light and load the hopper. Set the temperature to 225-250°F. Place your pork shoulder on the grill, close the lid and smoke it for 3 hours without opening the lid. Spray the shoulder generously with spray bottle mixture then continue to do so every hour for the next 3-4 hours until the shoulder reaches 200-205°F. Optionally, once the fat on top splits open, you may wrap the shoulder in butcher paper or aluminum foil for the duration of the cook. Remove from the smoker and allow it to rest for 1 hour before removing the bone and shredding. Enjoy!

Bacon Wrapped Kielbasa Bites

Cooking Time: 50 Min

Ingredients:

- 14 oz Kielbasa
- 12 oz bacon
- 8 oz BBQ sauce
- Fresh or dry parsley
- Your Favorite Rub

Directions:

1. Pre-heat grill to 350°
2. Slice kielbasa into 1" pieces or same size as the bacon strip.
3. Wrap bacon around the kielbasa.
4. Lightly coat the kielbasa bacon wrapped bites with Char-Griller Original Rub or your favorite rub.
5. Place the kielbasa bacon wrapped bites on your baking rack. Tip: spray rack with olive or vegetable spray to avoid sticking.
6. Next, put the baking rack with the kielbasa bacon bites in your grill at 350°F.
7. After 30 minutes or when bacon becomes golden brown begin to glaze the kielbasa bacon wrapped bites with bbq sauce to your liking.
8. Stick the kielbasa bacon wrapped bites with toothpicks for easy removal and easy handling to eat. Remove them from the grill.
9. Place in a serving tray or if tailgating, eat them right off the grill. Tip: serve with BBQ sauce on the side for dipping.
10. Enjoy!

Baby Back Ribs

Cooking Time: 3 Hrs

Ingredients:

- Salt
- Pepper
- Brown Sugar
- Garlic Salt
- Onion Salt
- Paprika

Directions:

1. Mix everything together and rub on ribs
2. Cover the ribs with foil and refrigerate overnight
3. Grill on 250° for 3 hours and take off
4. Throw your favorite BBQ sauce on and refold and grill till the BBQ sauce caramelizes. Take off and enjoy!

Brown Sugar Glazed Smoked Ham

Cooking Time: 2 Hrs

Ingredients:

- 11 lb. ham
- 1 C. brown sugar
- 1 C. brown mustard, or preferred

Directions:

1. Combine brown sugar and mustard together in a small bowl to make glaze. Mix well.
2. Score ham in a diamond pattern and generously brush on glaze.
3. Place glazed ham in large baking dish or cast-iron skillet onto the grill to smoke at 325°F for 2 hours. Ham is done when internal temperature reaches 140°F.
4. Remove ham from grill and let rest for 10 minutes before slicing and serving.

Bbq Burnt Ends

Cooking Time: 4.5 Hrs

Ingredients:

- 5-8lbs pork belly
- 1 - 1.5 C. BBQ sauce
- Favorite pork rub
- 1 stick of butter
- 1/3 C. of rum
- 1/3 C. brown sugar

Directions:

1. Trim top layer of fat
2. Cut into 2" wide vertical strips
3. Rotate and cut again to create 2" squares
4. Place in aluminum pan and season well with your favorite pork rub
5. Mix squares to thoroughly cover with rub
6. Heat grill to 250°F
7. Space out cubes evenly within grill
8. Let smoke for 3 hours at 250°F
9. Remove from grill and place in pan
10. Add 1.5 C. of your favorite BBQ sauce
11. Add 1/3 C. rum, 1/3 C. brown sugar, and 1 stick of butter
12. Mix well to evenly cover cubes
13. Smoke for another 1.5 - 1.75 hours

Flavor Pro Pork Steaks

Cooking Time: 12 Min

Ingredients:

- 4 Large Pork Steaks
- 1 Cup Stout Beer
- 2 Tbsp Canola Oil
- 3 Tbsp Minced Garlic
- 1/4 Cup Soy Sauce
- 2 Tbsp Worcestershire Sauce
- 1/3 Cup Packed Brown Sugar
- 2 tsp Hot Sauce
- 1 Tbsp Dijon Mustard
- 1 tsp Onion Powder
- 2 tsp Salt
- 2 tsp Pepper

Directions:

1. Add all ingredients to your favorite food-safe marinade container or ziplock bag along with the pork steaks.
2. Massage marinade into the steaks to ensure an even coating.
3. Store the container in the refrigerator for at least 2 hours but storing overnight is optimal.
4. Prepare the Flavor Pro for direct heat grilling (High, 400°F+) For best results, fill all three zones of the Flavor Drawer with charcoal and add a few wood chunks for added smoke flavor. Turn all four gas burners on high to ignite the coals,

once the coals are fully lit, turn off the gas completely. Leave both smoke stacks fully open.

5. Remove pork steaks from the marinade and place them on the grill directly over the coals.
6. Cook for 4-6 minutes per side.

Easter Sunday Texas-style Pulled Pork

Cooking Time: 8 Hrs

Ingredients:

- 6 to 7 Lb. Pork Shoulder
- 1/4 C. Kosher Salt
- 1/4 C. Coarse Black Pepper
- 2 Tbsp. Garlic Powder
- 2 Tbsp. Onion Powder
- 2 Tbsp. Paprika
- Hamburger Buns
- 1/2 C. Apple Juice (For Spritz)
- 1/2 C. Water (For Spritz)

Directions:

1. Easter Sunday is a time where we get together with family and friends. And what better way to feed all these people than with some Texas-style pulled pork sandwiches. Pulled pork really isn't a staple in Central-Texas BBQ but we love making it, and it feeds a lot of people. Your guests will be thanking you as they dive into some savory pork action!
2. Unwrap the pork shoulder and trim any excess fat or meat that may be hanging off.
3. You want to make it aerodynamic so the smoke flows evenly and does not create any burnt pieces.
4. Combine all dry ingredients in shaker for easy application.
5. Rub the pork shoulder down with olive oil or a binder of your choice. Season the pork shoulder liberally.
6. Get your grill up to 275°F and add a water pan to the side closest to the Side Fire Box.
7. This will allow for extra moisture inside the pit.
8. Once your grill is at 275°F you can go ahead and put the pork shoulder on. Let the pit do the work and tend to the fire as needed.
9. Tip: When preparing a fire, I usually use one large chimney of charcoal and add oak splits throughout the cook to maintain temp. The oak gives it that extra flavor you find in Central-Texas BBQ.
10. During the cook time is when I put my coleslaw together. Get the recipe here.
11. At around the 3-hour mark of the cook it is time to take-a-peek at the pork shoulder and spritz with the apple juice/water mixture to get some moisture on it.
12. Also, make sure that your water pan still has plenty of water left in it. Close the lid and keep on cooking.
13. Tip: Try to limit the amount of times you open the pit in order to limit fluctuations in temperature.
14. At around the 5-hour mark it is time to wrap the pork shoulder. Put it in an aluminum pan with some extra apple juice/water mixture to help with moisture.
15. Cover the pan with a layer of foil and put it back in the pit at 275°F.
16. Once the pork shoulder has reached 203°F (about 2-3 hours wrapped) it is time to take off the pit and let rest so the juices can redistribute.
17. Rest for 30-45 minutes.

18. Now is the moment of truth. Try to pull out the bone and if it gives little to no resistance then your pork shoulder is cooked to perfection!
19. Shred it and serve between a bun with a little coleslaw on top. Enjoy!

Oktoberfest Schweinebraten

Cooking Time: 30-40 Min

Ingredients:

- Boneless Pork Shoulder With Fat Cap and Skin
- 4-6 Cups Of Vegetable Broth
- 4 Carrots
- 4 Leeks
- 4 Celery Stalks
- 4 Medium Sized Onions
- 2 Bottles Of German Beer
- Salt & Pepper To Taste
- 3 Tbsp Butter

Directions:

1. Lay shoulder fat side down in a roasting pan Pour in enough vegetable broth to keep the fat cap covered Place on the grill at 300F for 30-40 minutes. This will help soften the skin. Cut up your vegetables into 1-2" lengths. Cut the onions into chunks Remove the meat from grill and set aside for next step Butter up your roasting pan and fill with your cut up vegetables. Brown the vegetables slightly Cut 1/2" or 1cm cubes into the fat cap being careful not to cut into the meat. Season with salt and pepper and get it down into the cube crevices. Pour the vegetable broth on top of your browned vegetables not too much, just enough to cover them. Place your seasoned shoulder on top of the vegetable bed Pour 2 bottles of your favorite dark german beer over shoulder and vegetables Raise grill heat to 340-350F and cook until internal temp of 160-165F checking throughout. Cut up and enjoy!

Hoppin' John

Cooking Time: 15 Min

Ingredients:

- 2 Tbsp. Olive oil
- ½ C. onion, diced
- ¾ C. bell pepper, diced
- 15 oz. can black-eyed peas
- Salt and pepper, to taste
- ¼ lb. smoked pulled pork
- Chipotle peppers
- 2 C. cooked white rice
- Andouille sausage

Directions:

1. Pre-heat grill to 350°F and place a 10" cast iron skillet on grill and heat until very hot. 2. Place sausages on the grill and allow to cook for 8-10 minutes, turning once or twice, until cooked through. 3. Pour 2 Tbsp. olive oil into hot skillet and add onion, bell pepper and black-eyed peas. 4. Season with salt and pepper and allow to cook for 1-2 minutes, stirring occasionally. 5. Add smoked pulled pork and Chipotle peppers and stir. 6. Add cooked rice to mixture. Close lid and allow to cook for 3-4 minutes. 7. Add grilled andouille sausage from Step
2. Remove from grill and serve. Enjoy!

Blueberry Pork Belly Burnt Ends

Cooking Time: 3.5 Hrs

Ingredients:

- Pork Belly - 2 lbs
- Char-Griller Rib Rub
- Butter - 1/2 stick
- Fresh Blueberries - 2 Cups

- Apple Juice - 1/4 Cup
- Sugar - 1/4 Cup
- Cornstarch - 1 Tbs
- Lemon Juice - 1 Tbs
- Cayenne - 1 tsp (optional)

Directions:

1. Cut the pork belly into 1-1 ½ inch cubes.
2. Season the cubes liberally on all sides.
3. Prepare the fire to get the smoker up to 275 F.
4. Tip: Put the pork belly into the freezer 20-30 minutes before you cube. This will help with the cutting process.
5. Once the smoker has reached 275 F put the pork belly onto the grill with the fat side facing down.
6. Spritz every 40-45 minutes until the pork belly starts to read an internal temp of 190 F.
7. Place the cubes in an aluminum pan and add one cup of the blueberry sauce and the butter. Toss the cubes to make sure the sauce adheres to all sides of the cubes. Return the pan into the smoker.
8. Once the sauce has reduced and the cubes look caramelized it is time to pull from the smoker. Put the burnt ends onto a plate and top with the remaining cup of blueberry sauce. Enjoy!
9. In a saucepan combine the blueberries and apple juice. Bring to a boil. Pour the cornstarch, sugar, and cayenne (optional) into the saucepan while stirring continuously. Let the sauce thicken and reduce heat. Add the lemon juice and stir. Set aside till it is time to use on the burnt ends.
10. Serving Suggestion: Over Homemade Waffles

Chipotle Orange Glazed Bacon Wrapped And Stuffed Pork Loin

Cooking Time: 2 Hrs

Ingredients:

- 1-1½ lb. pork tenderloins
- 1 lb. bacon
- 1 C. spicy honey BBQ sauce
- 1 C. sweet orange marmalade
- 1 Tbsp. crushed fresh garlic, to taste
- 1 Tbsp. Chipotle chili powder, to taste
- 3 Tbsp. pork rub or preferred seasoning

Directions:

1. Combine BBQ sauce, marmalade, garlic and Chipotle chili powder in a saucepan on the stove until heated through, 3-5 minutes or until all ingredients are well blended. 2. Mix well and turn heat to low until ready to use. 3. Stir occasionally and refrigerate leftovers.
2. Pork tenderloin
3. Generously season pork tenderloins with rub and layer 2-3 strips of bacon on top. 2. Evenly spread a ¼ of the Chipotle orange glaze over the bacon layer. Tie securely in multiple spots with kitchen twine. Snip off any excess twine. 4. Lay out remaining bacon in a basket weave pattern on a cutting board. 5. Wrap the pork tenderloin, tucking ends under and season with rub. 6. Place bacon wrapped tenderloin to smoke on the indirect side of the grill at 225°F for 2 hours. 7. Brush the remaining Chipotle orange glaze onto the pork tenderloin during the last ½ hour of smoking. Pork is ready when the internal temperature reaches 165°F. Note: The tenderloin's internal temperature will continue to increase by 5-10 degrees after you pull it off the grill.

Certified Grilled And Smoked Baby Back Ribs

Cooking Time: 2 1/2 Hrs

Ingredients:

- Full Slabs of Spare Ribs.
- Hot Sauce
- Favorite BBQ Rub
- Favorite BBQ Sauce
- Apple Juice (Non Concentrate)

Directions:

1. Trimming
2. Using a sharp knife slice remove any meat loose on the ends of the ribs. Also remove any access fat from top/meat side of the ribs.Tip: If you can pull any fat, you should remove it.
3. Flip the ribs over so the bones are facing up. Remove the membrane and discard. Remove any access fat.
4. Seasoning
5. Begin by leaving the the ribs bone side up. Apply coating of hot sauce for a binder.Tip: don't apply hot sauce or rubs on the sides of the ribs. This helps the exposed bones from getting burnt during the smoking process.
6. Apply even coating of BBQ rubs on the ribs.
7. Flip ribs to the top/meat side of the ribs. Apply coating of hot sauce for a binder.Tip: seasoning the bottom of the ribs first will help prevent the top/meat side seasonings from being messy.
8. Apply an even coating of BBQ rub on the top of the ribs.
9. Ribs are ready to be Smoked.
10. Grilling & Smoking
11. Grill the ribs for 2 minutes on the meat side down on the grill grill grate. Reverse them after one minute.
12. Flip the ribs so they meat side is facing up and grill for an additional 1-2 minutes.
13. Using your Char-Griller Grill glove and grill grate lifter, lift the grill grate and move off to the side of the grill. Quickly insert the Char-Griller Akorn Smokin' stone, insert Char-Griller grill drip pan filled with water, place grill grate with meat back in the pit.
14. Shut the top smoke stack to a low setting and dodge same to the bottom of the vent. This will allow you to quickly lower your fire. Lock in the temperature when it hits temperature 325°-350° by adjusting the smoke stack and bottom vent.
15. Spritz with apple juice every 30 minutes and rotate ribs.
16. After smoking for 2 1/2 hours coat ribs with BBQ sauce and smoke for an additional 20 minutes.
17. Remove Ribs and allow to rest for 15 minutes. Slice and enjoy.

Quick And Easy Grilled Pork Tenderloin

Cooking Time: 25 Min

Ingredients:

- 1 Pork Tenderloin
- 1 Tsp Paprika
- 1/2 Tsp Garlic Powder
- 1/2 Tsp Cilantro
- 1/2 Tsp Oregano
- Salt and Pepper to Taste
- Olive Oil

Directions:

1. Blend spices together in a bowl. Rub pork with olive oil and then season liberally on both sides with spice blend. Set up the Flavor Pro™ for direct cooking. Ignite burners and turn to medium high. Place pork on the grill and cook for 8 to 10 minutes per side or until the internal temperature reads 165 degrees. Remove from grill and let rest for 10 minutes.

Memphis-style Dry Ribs

Cooking Time: 5 Hrs

Ingredients:

- 3 racks of ribs
- Ribs BBQ rub, to taste
- Apple juice
- Brown sugar
- Honey
- 12 oz. bottle of squeeze butter

Directions:

1. Rinse rib racks and pat dry with paper towel. Remove membrane from each rack by carefully prying back using the back of a sharp knife. Discard membrane. Flip racks and trim loose ends and excess fat.
2. Tip: Use a paper towel to help hold the membrane, as it's slippery.
3. Season ribs generously with Ribs BBQ Rub, or your favorite rub.
4. When setting up the grill, use a full chimney of unlit charcoal in the attached Side Fire Box and pour another ½ chimney of hot coals on top to ensure good smoke and a temperature of 275°F. Add Applewood chunks on top.
5. Adjust the charcoal grate to the highest setting in the main compartment. Place an aluminum pan on the grate and fill halfway with apple juice. Smoke ribs for 1 hour and mist with apple juice. Close lid and smoke for another 3 hours.
6. After 3 hours, remove ribs from grill and wrap. Before wrapping, spread a generous layer of brown sugar, butter and honey onto aluminum foil. Place ribs meat side down and wrap securely.
7. Transfer wrapped ribs to the grill and smoke at 275°F for another hour. Carefully drain juices before slicing and serving.

Father's Day Baby Back Ribs

Cooking Time: 6 Hrs

Ingredients:

- 1 C. warmed honey
- 1/2 C. yellow or Dijon mustard
- 2 oz. brown sugar
- 1 oz smoked paprika
- 1 Tbsp. black pepper
- 1 Tsp. crushed red pepper flakes
- 2 C. water
- 2 oz chipotle peppers

Directions:

1. Mix mustard and honey in small bowl
2. Pour over ribs and coat evenly
3. Mix together brown sugar, black pepper, red pepper flakes, and paprika in a bowl
4. Coat ribs generously with the rub mix
5. Wrap in aluminum foil and leave in the refrigerator for 24 hours
6. Pre heat grill to 275° F
7. Mix 2 C. of water and 2 oz. of chipotle peppers in a cast iron skillet
8. Baste with liquid in skillet every hour
9. Smoke for about 6 hours or until internal temperature reaches 175° F

How To: Easy Dry Rub Grilled Pork Tenderloin

Ingredients:

- 1.5 Lbs Pork Tenderloin (Trimmed and Pat Dry)
- 1 Tbsp Brown Sugar
- 1 Tbsp Garlic Powder
- 1 Tbsp Chili Powder
- 1 Tbsp Salt
- 1 Tbsp Black Pepper
- 1 Tsp Smoked Paprika
- 1 Tsp Red Chili Flake

Directions:

1. Preheat Char-Griller Grill to high heat. For an easy weeknight dinner, I use the gas side of my Texas Trio for quick cooking, but of course, charcoal flavor would only add to this recipe! While grill is heating, mix spices together, sprinkle heavily over the meat, and rub well. Allow the meat to sit at room temperature for about 20 minutes, letting the spices marry. When grill has reached high heat, add pork loin and close lid. In 5 minutes, rotate meat clockwise to make diamond marks, and allow to cook another 5 minutes with the lid closed. After 10 minutes on one side has passed, flip your pork, and repeat- 5 minutes in one position with the lid closed, and rotate again, 5 minutes with the lid closed. I like to pull my pork off the grill at 145 degrees. While it rests, it will come up about 5-8 more degrees, allowing the meat to stay perfectly moist. Remove meat from the grill, cover loosely with foil, and let rest for 15 minutes before slicing. Serve with your favorite grilled vegetable or a large tossed salad. Enjoy!

Raspberry Chipotle Glazed Pork Tenderloin

Cooking Time: 35 Min

Ingredients:

- 2 Lb Pork Tenderloin
- 1 tsp Mustard
- 1 Tbsp Char-Griller Rib Rub
- 3/4 Cup Raspberry Chipotle BBQ Sauce

Directions:

1. Pre-heat the grill to 325 F and set up for cooking with indirect heat
2. Trim excess fat off the pork tenderloin.
3. Rub down with a light coating of mustard to help the rub stick.
4. Season all sides of the pork tenderloin with Char-Griller Rib Rub
5. Once the grill has reached 325 F place the pork tenderloin on the grill in indirect heat.
6. Once the pork tenderloin has reached an internal temp of 140 F it is time to apply the glaze.
7. Heat up the raspberry chipotle sauce and use a brush to apply the glaze on the pork tenderloin.
8. Once the glaze has set and the internal temp of the pork tenderloin has reached 145 F it is time to pull off the grill and let rest for 10 minutes.
9. Slice and serve with extra raspberry chipotle sauce for dipping. Enjoy!

Bacon Wrapped Kabob

Cooking Time: 10 Min

Ingredients:

- 1 Lb KC Cattle Company (Wagyu Stew or Kabob Meat)
- 10 Strips of Bacon (Cut In Half)

- 1 Tsp Redmond Real Salt
- 1 Tsp Redmond Organic Garlic Pepper

Directions:

1. Season beef with salt & pepper, wrap each piece with bacon & skewer them. Cook on flat iron griddle (or grill) turning every 2 minutes, for 10 minutes. I finished mine off in the air fryer to crisp the bacon up a little more without over cooking the beef.

Asian Pork Belly Skewers

Cooking Time: 2 Hrs

Ingredients:

- Pork Belly Cut into 1 1/2" Cubes - 2 Pounds
- Pineapple Cut into 1 1/2" Cubes - 1
- Char-Griller Rib Rub
- Skewers Soaked in Water
- Chopped Green Onions and Sesame Seeds - For Garnish
- Chili Garlic Sauce - 1 Tablespoon
- Rice Wine Vinegar - 1 Teaspoon
- Chopped Garlic - 1 Teaspoon
- Orange Zest - 1 Teaspoon
- Soy Sauce - 2 Teaspoons

Directions:

1. Light grill for indirect heat
2. In a large bowl, toss pork belly with rub until generously coated
3. Skewer pineapple and pork belly, alternating between the two
4. Please skewers on the grill
5. Rotate skewers after an hour
6. Meanwhile, place all sauce ingredients in a small sauce pan
7. Chili Garlic Sauce Rice Wine Vinegar Chopped Garlic Range Zest Soy Sauce Honey Ground Ginger
8. Bring the sauce to a simmer and allow to cook until thickened. Approximately 15 minutes
9. Allow to cool
10. After two hours, brush the skewers with sauce. Allow the sauce to set for approximately 30 minutes
11. When ready to serve, sprinkle with sesame seeds and green onions

BEEF

Foil Packet Short Ribs

Cooking Time: 1.5 To 2.5 Hrs

Ingredients:

- Packed Brown Sugar - 1 Tbs
- Paprika - 1 Tbs
- Chili Powder - 1 Tbs
- Salt - 1 tsp
- Garlic Powder - 1 tsp
- 4 Pounds of Beef Short Ribs
- Barbecue Sauce of Choice - 1/2 Cup
- Ice Cubes

Directions:

1. Mix together sugar, chili powder, salt and garlic powder
2. Rub the meat with the mixture generously
3. Place ribs in a dish, cover and put in fridge for 30 minutes
4. Preheat grill to medium indirect heat.
5. Center ¼ of the ribs and two ice cubes on a sheet of foil, seal the packet allowing room for air to circulate.
6. Repeat for three more packets
7. Grill packets over medium, 375 to 400, indirect heat for 1 and a half to two hours or until tender.
8. Open packets and brush ribs with barbecue sauce, cover and grill over indirect heat for 5 minutes. Turning the ribs once.
9. Serve with additional sauce as desired.

Bbq Fiends Beef Fajitas

Cooking Time: 8 Min

Ingredients:

- 1 Lb Skirt Steak
- 1 Tbsp Char-Griller Steak Seasoning
- 1/2 Cup Orange Juice (Marinade)
- 1/4 Cup White Onion (Marinade)
- 1 Jalapeno, Seeds Removed (Marinade)
- 1 Habanero, Seeds Removed (Marinade)
- 4 Garlic Cloves (Marinade)
- 1 Tbsp Olive Oil
- 1 Lime, Juiced (Marinade)
- Pinch of Salt & Pepper (Marinade)

Directions:

1. Combine all marinade ingredients in a blender and lightly pulse
2. Place skirt steak in a Ziploc bag with the marinade. Make sure the marinade is covering all sides of the fajitas. *Tip* leave the fajitas refrigerated in the marinade for 1-2 hours for increased flavor.
3. Remove the fajitas from the marinade and lightly season with Char-Griller steak seasoning on both sides. Get the grill up to 375 F and place the fajitas over the direct heat. Grill for 3-4 minutes on each side for medium rare.
4. Pull the fajitas and let rest for 5 minutes. Slice against the grain and serve with tortillas. Enjoy!

Smoked Chili

Cooking Time: 2-3 Hrs

Ingredients:

- 2 lb. ground beef
- 30 oz. tomato sauce
- 30 oz. kidney beans
- 30 oz. pinto beans
- 1 C. diced onion
- ¼ C. diced green chilies

- 3 medium tomatoes chopped
- 1½ Tsp. cumin powder
- 3 Tbsp. chili powder
- 2 Tsp. black pepper
- 1 Tsp. salt
- 1 Tsp. celery salt
- 2-4 cloves garlic, minced
- ½ C. chopped cilantro
- 2 C. water

Directions:

1. Pre-heat grill to 250°F. Season ground beef with salt and pepper, to taste and brown in a cast iron pan.
2. Mix all ingredients together, add to browned ground beef and stir well to combine.
3. Smoke for 2-3 hours at 250°F, stirring every 15-20 minutes.

Flat Iron Sausage And Peppers Hash

Cooking Time: 10 Min

Ingredients:

- 1 Pound Of Ground Sausage
- 1 Red Pepper (Chopped)
- 1 Green Pepper (Chopped)
- 1 White Onion (Chopped)
- 1-2 Large Potatoes Chopped Into Small Cubes
- Eggs (Optional)

Directions:

1. Heat the Flat Iron to medium heat. Add oil to the flat top. Cook ground sausage until well browned and move to the side. Add potatoes to allow them time to begin cooking first. Cook potatoes until they begin to brown/ ¾ of the way done. Use spatulas to push them to the side. Add more oil if necessary then add onions and peppers. Cook them until they begin to soften. Push those to the side with the potatoes. Mix all dish components together on the Flat Iron together and cook to your liking. Serve hot. Optionally add eggs to the dish at the end, especially if serving as a breakfast dish. Enjoy!

Smoked Beef Ribs

Cooking Time: 7-10 Hrs

Ingredients:

- 1 4-5 lb. Rack Of Beef Ribs
- Water and Apple Cider Vinegar in a spray bottle
- 2 Tbsp of Kosher Salt
- 2 Tbsp of Ground Black Pepper
- 1 Tsp of Brown Sugar
- 1 Tsp of Brown Sugar
- 1 Tsp of Brown Sugar
- 1 Tsp of Cayenne Pepper

Directions:

1. Alternatively, you can use your favorite pre-mixed rub/seasoning.
2. Preheat your smoker to 225-250°F. Thoroughly mix the rub ingredients together. Ensure your ribs are as dry as possible for the crispiest exterior. Pat dry with paper towels if necessary. Coat the exterior of your ribs in the rub mix, massaging it with hands to make sure it is thoroughly rubbed into the meat. Place the ribs into the smoker, fat side up with a water pan underneath close to the Side Fire Box. Close the lids and allow to smoke for 2-3 hours before beginning to spritz with water/vinegar mixture every hour until internal temperature reaches 200-203°F. This process should be 7-10 hours depending on the rack. Remove the ribs from the smoker and wrap in butcher paper, allowing them to rest for an hour before slicing and serving.

Shrimp & Sausage Skewers

Cooking Time: 5 Min

Ingredients:

- 4 Smoked Sausage Links or Hot links
- 20 Large Shrimp
- 2-3 Tbsp Blackening seasoning (I used Ashman Co Bayou Blackening)
- 1/4 Cup Teriyaki Sauce

Directions:

1. Preheat grill to 400F
2. Peel and de-vein shrimp, slice links into 5 pieces each.
3. Wrap shrimp around sausage link and put on skewer.
4. Once all shrimp and sausage are on skewers, sprinkle with blackening seasoning.
5. Place on grill for approximately 3-4 minutes per side, just enough to get a good char.
6. Once cooked baste both sides with teriyaki sauce, remove from grill and serve!

Smokin' Champ Smoked Beef Back Ribs

Cooking Time: 5-6 Hrs

Ingredients:

- 2 Beef Back Ribs
- Mustard
- Fogo Charcoal The Rub
- Foil
- Apple Juice For Spritzer and Wrap With.
- Char-Griller Grills Smokin' Champ 1624 & Drip Pan
- Fogo Quebracho Lump Charcoal

Directions:

1. Trim any fat and silver skin from the top and bottom of the Beef Back Ribs. Apply even coating of mustard to the top and bottom. Season the top and bottom of the meat with Fogo Charcoal The Rub. Tip: Allow ribs to get to room temperature prior to smoking. This allows the seasonings to sweat and absorb into the meat and the meat will begin to smoke faster. Prep your Char-Griller Grill Smokin' Champ 1624 with drip pan filled with water. Fire up your Char-Griller Grill Smokin' Champ 1624 to temperature 250°: used Fogo Quebracho Lump Charcoal & Mesquite Mini Wood Logs. Spritz with apple juice every hour minutes during the smoking process and rotate the ribs each time. Place ribs in your Char-Griller Grill Smokin' Champ 1624 and smoke until internal temperature 170° is met, roughly takes 3-4 hours. Tip: remember to use your Char-Griller Grills folding probe to take the guess work out your cooking. Wrap with foil and apple juice once internal temperature 170° is met. Place back in the Char-Griller Grill Smokin' Champ 1624 and cook until internal temperature 199° is met, roughly takes 1 hour 30 minutes to get from internal temperature 170° to internal temperature 199° Remove from the smoker and allow to rest in a cooler covered with a towel/blanket for 1-2hours. Remove, slice and enjoy!

Lou's Beef Brisket

Cooking Time: 10-12 Hrs

Ingredients:

- 15-18 lb. beef brisket
- ½ C. coarse ground pepper
- ½ C. Kosher salt
- Beef broth for injection

Directions:

1. Use the rub ingredients to sprinkle the brisket on all sides to your taste
2. Inject the brisket with the combined ingredients of the injection
3. Use half the combined ingredients for injection and other half for misting
4. Add in your favorite wood chips/chunks (hickory, cherry, etc.)
5. Place brisket onto your smoker, fat side up
6. Cook for three hours in the smoker at 250°F, open it and inject again without turning the brisket 8. Use some of the inject to mist the exposed surface generously 9. Remove brisket when internal temperature reaches 160°F and wrap tightly in foil 10. Return brisket to grill and cook until the internal meat temperature reaches 204°F 11. Remove from heat and allow it to rest for an hour before slicing and serving

Lou's Beef Plate Ribs

Cooking Time: 7 Hrs

Ingredients:

- 1 rack, three bones, Beef Plate Ribs (approx. 6-9 pounds)
- ½ C. coarse ground black pepper
- ¼ C. Kosher salt
- 2 C. beef broth

Directions:

1. Sprinkle liberally with the salt and black pepper mixture, coating lightly over all sides
2. Pre-heat your grill to 275°F
3. Place the ribs on the top rack and smoke for 6 hours at 275°F
4. Mist about every 2 hours with some beef broth in a spray bottle
5. At the end of the 6 hours remove from the smoker and allow to rest for 30 minutes to an hour, then cut and serve

Bbq Fiends Barbacoa Tacos

Cooking Time: 5 Hrs

Ingredients:

- Beef Cheeks - 2 to 3 lbs
- Kosher Salt - 1 Tbsp
- Coarse Black Pepper - 1 Tbsp
- Olive Oil - 1 tsp
- Beef Broth (Low Sodium) - 2 Cups
- 1 White Onion
- Tortillas - 12
- Cilantro (optional)

Directions:

1. Combine salt and pepper in a shaker for easy application. Unwrap beef cheeks and trim excess fat and silver skin off the meat.
2. Rub down the meat with olive oil for a binder and season evenly with your salt/pepper mixture.
3. Start working on getting the fire going and your smoker up to 275 F. Once your smoker is at 275 F you can add a water pan to the side of your grill that is closest to the fire. This will help with keeping your beef cheeks moist. Center the beef cheeks on the middle of the grill and let the smoker do the work.
4. Once the beef cheeks have reached around 165 F internal temp it is time to braise (this should be around the 3-hour mark).
5. Apply a layer of onion slices to the bottom of an aluminum pan. Set your beef cheeks on top of the layer of onions.
6. Carefully pour the beef broth into the pan and make sure to cover the pan completely with aluminum foil.

7. Put the pan back into the smoker and continue to maintain a temperature of 275 F.

8. Once the beef cheeks have reached an internal temp between 203-205 F it is time to take them off the smoker and let rest for 10 minutes. The beef cheeks should be very tender and falling apart when probed.

9. After the beef cheeks have rested for 10 minutes inside of the pan it is time to remove them from the pan and shred them on a cutting board.

10. Once your barbacoa is all shredded go ahead and fill your tortillas with the delicious meat and serve with diced onions and cilantro!

11. Enjoy your barbacoa tacos with your family and friends!

Double Cheeseburger Kabobs

Cooking Time: 30 Min

Ingredients:

- Grass Fed Ground Beef- 1 Pound
- Sea Salt
- Fresh Ground Pepper
- American Cheese Slices
- Dill Pickle Chips
- Iceberg Lettuce
- Small Vine Cherry Tomatoes

Directions:

1. Gently form the ground beef into small slider size patties and generously sprinkle both sides with salt and pepper. Grill over medium high heat until desired doneness and then melt a quarter of a slice of American cheese on top of each.

2. Cut the iceberg lettuce into small squares. Slide a cooked slider patty, pickle chip, lettuce square, and tomato onto a skewer. Repeat twice on each skewer. 3. Serve with sugar free ketchup and yellow mustard to dip.

3. Other options to add: cooked bacon, red onion, grilled mushrooms—get creative!

Bacon Cheeseburger Pizza-dough Balls

Cooking Time: 30 Min

Ingredients:

- 22oz pizza dough
- 1.5 Lb Ground Beef
- 15 Slices Cheddar Cheese
- Half a Pack Of Bacon
- Seasonings
- 2 Eggs
- Sesame seeds

Directions:

1. Using your Flat Iron and your charcoal grill, accomplish the perfect game day appetizer or fun weeknight finger food with these bacon cheeseburger pizza dough balls. Rob Kennedy of Mr. Homeowner has got you covered with yet another fun and easy family friendly recipe!

2. Take your ground beef and make approx 15 little patties Cook your patties and bacon on your griddle about halfway cooked Wrap cheese, bacon and mini-patty in some pizza dough Cover with egg wash and some sesame seeds Set grill to 350F and 'bake' indirect heat for 25-30 minutes Enjoy!

Mac & Cheese Stuffed Meatballs On The Char-griller Akorn

Cooking Time: 20 Min

Ingredients:

- 2-3 lbs 80/20 Ground Beef
- 1 Cup Shredded Cheddar Cheese
- 2/3 cup Panco Bread Crumbs
- Ground Black Pepper
- Your Favorite BBQ Sauce
- Velveta Mac & Cheese (Or Homemade)

Directions:

1. Cook up the Mac & Cheese Mix up ground beef, cheese, bread crumbs and pepper in a bowl Make little meat plates (3-4" in diameter) Place 4-5 noodles in each 'plate' Wrap the meat around the noodles so they're in the middle of a ball Heat up grill (indirect) to 350-375F Cook for 15 minutes Move around so everyone gets a turn Cook another 10-15 minutes, paint on some BBQ sauce Cook another 5 or so minutes to get tacky Enjoy!

Grilled Steak Caesar Salad

Cooking Time: 30 Min

Ingredients:

- Hanger or Flank Steak (12 oz)
- Large Head of Romaine Lettuce
- 1/2 Baguette, Cut into Large Cubes
- 1/3 Cup Shaved Parmesan
- 1 Tbsp Olive Oil
- Salt and Pepper to Taste
- Juice of One Lemon (Dressing)
- 1 Tbsp Worcestershire Sauce (Dressing)
- 1 Tbsp Anchovy Paste (Dressing)
- 2 Cloves Fresh Garlic (Dressing)
- 1/2 Cup Grated Parmesan (Dressing)
- 1 Egg Yolk (Dressing)
- 1 Tbsp Dijon (Dressing)
- Salt and Pepper to Taste (Dressing)

Directions:

1. Cut washed romaine in half, and toss cubed baguette with a drizzle of olive oil, salt and pepper.
2. Once grill is heated to 500+, lay steak on clean grates, and add romaine cut side down, and crouton cubes as well. Turn croutons every 1-2 minutes, until they're golden brown.
3. Pull romaine and croutons from grill, and allow steak to cook evenly on both sides. I like my steak medium-rare, so I cooked each piece for 4 minutes per side.
4. Pull the steak and allow to rest for 15 minutes.
5. While your steak is resting, blend all the dressing ingredients except for the olive oil until a paste forms.
6. Then, with the blender running on low, slowly drizzle in the oil until well combined and thick- you know what caesar dressing should look like!
7. Chop grilled romaine, slice steak, and assemble on your salad plate, sprinkling with the grilled croutons and shaved parmesan. Drizzle the dressing over the top, and you've got dinner ready to go! Enjoy, friends!

Leftover Brisket Nachos

Cooking Time: 20 Min

Ingredients:

- Tortilla Chips
- Leftover Brisket
- Shredded Cheddar and Monterey Jack Cheese
- Heavy Cream

- Canned Diced Chilis
- Sour Cream
- Limes
- Pickled Jalapenos
- Black Beans
- Avocados
- Radish
- Pico De Gallo: Tomatoes, Onion, Jalapeno, Cilantro

Directions:

1. Prepare your pico de gallo and guacamole
2. Combine diced tomato, jalapeno, onion and cilantro in a bowl and mix with salt and pepper and lime juice
3. Mash 2 avocados together and combine with ½ cup of the pico for some easy guacamole
4. In a skillet prepare the cheese sauce by adding 3 cups shredded cheese and 2 cans of diced chilis. Slowly mix in ½ cup heavy cream and stir until smooth
5. Reheat your leftover brisket in another skillet
6. On a large cookie sheet begin layering your nachos
7. Chips, brisket, black beans, cheese sauce, more chips, brisket, beans cheese sauce.
8. ALWAYS double layer the nachos when possible
9. Top with pico de gallo, pickled jalapenos, sour cream, and guacamole!
10. Garnish with radish and lime wedges and enjoy!

Chili In A Bread Bowl

Ingredients:

- 2 Lbs Ground Beef
- 8 Hot Link Sausages
- 8 Hot Italian Sausage
- 5 McCormick Mild Chili Seasoning Packets
- 2 Red Onions
- 1 Red Bell Pepper
- 1 Green Bell Pepper
- 2 Jalapenos
- 4 Garlic Cloves
- 4 10oz Cans of Diced Tomatoes and Green Chilies
- 2 Cans Pinto Beans
- 2 Cans Red Kidney Beans
- Shredded Cheese
- Bread Loaf (Bread Bowls)

Directions:

1. Chop your green pepper, red pepper, and red onion Using the Side Burner on our Triple Play, cook ground beef with diced garlic and jalapenos in a large pot Once the beef is cooked, add the 4 cans of diced tomatoes and green chilies Add the 4 cans of beans and mix to combine Add the 5 McCormick seasoning packets Now that your sausages are charred, slice them all and add to the pot Simmer for 30-45 minutes Hollow out your bread loaf with a paring knife to create the bowls Serve in the bread bowls and top with shredded cheese and raw red onions (or whatever else you like!)
2. Pitt Tips: Spice it up a little more by adding your favorite hot sauce, we like Tapatio! Add even more flavor by adding in your favorite beer!

Shrimp 'n Grits

Cooking Time: 20-25 Min

Ingredients:

- 1 lb. shrimp, peeled and deveined
- ½ lb. andouille sausage
- 1 C. stone-ground yellow grits
- 3 Tbsp. butter

- 4 C. water
- 2 C. shredded sharp Cheddar cheese
- 4 Tsp. lemon juice
- 2 Tbsp. parsley, chopped
- 1 C. scallions, thinly sliced
- 1 large garlic clove, minced
- Olive oil
- Salt and pepper, to taste

Directions:

1. Pre-heat grill to 375°F. Bring water to a boil and add salt and pepper, to taste. Add grits and cook until water is absorbed, about 20- 25 minutes. Remove from heat, stir in butter and cheese. 2. While grits are cooking, place sausages on the indirect side of the grill for 10-12 minutes, turning occasionally, until cooked. Sausage is done when internal temperature reaches 160°F. Remove from grill, allow to cool and roughly chop. 3. Rinse shrimp and pat dry with paper towel. Season with olive oil, salt and pepper, to taste. Grill shrimp for 2 minutes on each side, until opaque. 4. Remove shrimp from grill and toss with parsley, lemon juice, scallions and garlic.
2. To serve, spoon grits into bowls, top with chopped andouille sausage, and place shrimp on top of sausage. Garnish with more scallions and enjoy!

Smoked Mexican Burgers

Cooking Time: 40-45 Min

Ingredients:

- 2 lbs. ground beef
- ½ lb. Chorizo or spicy Italian sausage
- Jalapeños or Poblano peppers, halved, cored and seeded
- Sriracha or Chipotle aioli sauce
- Cheese slices
- Condiments of choice
- Hamburger buns
- Salt and pepper, to taste

Directions:

1. Pre-heat grill to 225°F and set up for indirect heat, with charcoal to one side.
2. Combine ground beef and Chorizo or spicy Italian sausage together in a large bowl and mix by hand until just blended. Season to taste with salt and pepper.
3. Form 1" thick patties and place on the indirect side of the grill, away from the heat source. Smoke until internal temperature reaches 130°F. Add peppers alongside the burgers and smoke for 40-45 minutes.
4. Increase heat to 400°F. Remove the peppers from the grill and set aside. When grill is at temperature, transfer burgers to the direct heat side. Sear for 6 minutes per side with a quarter turn halfway through.
5. Add cheese and allow to melt, 2-3 minutes. Burgers are done when internal temperature reaches 160°F.
6. Place cheese burger on bun, add peppers and sauce. Top with condiments of choice. Serve and enjoy!

Filet Mignon, Risotto, And Asparagus

Cooking Time: 20 Min

Ingredients:

- 1 C. Arborio rice
- 2 C. chicken stock
- 1 C. water
- 4 oz. heavy cream
- 4 oz. shredded Parmesan cheese
- 1/2 shallot, minced

- 1 bunch asparagus
- 1 lemon, sliced in half
- 2 oz. olive oil
- 6oz. filets
- 2 garlic cloves, minced
- Salt and pepper to taste
- A pinch of saffron (optional)

Directions:

1. Butter cast iron skillet over grill heat
2. Add minced shallot and garlic, and sauté for 30-45 seconds until fragrant
3. Add rice and sauté for 1 minute
4. Add 1½ cups of chicken stock, setting aside remaining ½ cup
5. Add 1 cup of water
6. Cook for 10 minutes, stirring frequently
7. Add remaining ½ cup chicken stock, and cook for additional 10 minutes
8. Season to taste with salt and pepper
9. Add a pinch of saffron (optional)
10. Slowly add heavy cream
11. Remove from heat and stir in shredded Parmesan cheese
12. Filet Mignon
13. Season generously with salt and pepper 2. Place filets on grill at 400°F for 5-7 minutes on each side for medium-rare 3. Top filets with slice of butter until melted
14. Asparagus
15. Add raw asparagus and grill for 2-5 minutes 2. Squeeze lemon juice over asparagus 3. Drizzle with olive oil 4. Spread minced garlic 5. Add salt and pepper to taste 6. Mix garlic, salt, and pepper with tongs to evenly coat asparagus 7. Cook for 3-5 minutes, depending on thickness

Steak Night! Steak, Shrimp And Asparagus On The Akorn

Cooking Time: 20 Min

Ingredients:

- NY Strip Steaks
- Asparagus
- Raw shrimp
- Salt & Pepper
- 2 Lemons
- Minced Garlic
- Olive Oil
- Shrimp seasoning (we used Uncle Steve's Shake - gator shake)

Directions:

1. Pat your steak dry and cover with a thin coat of olive oil Cover all sides with some salt and pepper Let the steak sit on the counter while you get the shrimp and asparagus ready Peel the shrimp place on skewers and cover with your favorite seasoning Cut the woody portion off the bottom of the asparagus, coat with oil and season with salt, pepper, minced garlic. Squeeze some lemon juice over Bring your grill up to 500F and place your steaks on there no diffuser plate. After 2 minutes, twist 45 degrees After 2 minutes, flip After 2 minutes twist 45 degrees After 2 minutes temp probe and let cook until 130F internal for medium rare Pull steak and let it rest room temp while you cook your shrimp and asparagus With grill still at 500F, place shrimp skewers on grill Place asparagus directly on grill as well single file if possible Keep an eye on these flip the shrimp after about 3 minutes and move the asparagus around. Cook until desired doneness shrimp should be 145F if you would like to be safe. Enjoy!

Chili Jalapeño Burger

Cooking Time: 10 Min

Ingredients:

- ½ C. mayonnaise
- ½ Tsp. ground white pepper
- 1 Tsp. garlic powder
- 1 Tsp. Chipotle chili powder
- 2 lbs. ground beef
- 2 eggs, beaten
- 1 ½ C. all-purpose beef sauce (reserve ½ C.)
- 1 Tbsp. Steak BBQ rub
- 15 oz. can chili, preferred (without beans)
- 2-3 jalapeños, sliced
- Hamburger buns
- Cheddar cheese slices
- Condiments of choice

Directions:

1. Combine the mayonnaise, white pepper, garlic powder, Chipotle chili powder and ½ C. of reserved sauce in a small bowl. Mix thoroughly. 2. Cover with plastic wrap and place it in the refrigerator for 30 minutes to chill.
2. Ground beef
3. Place ground beef in large bowl, add eggs and season with 1 Tbsp. Steak BBQ rub, or your favorite rub, to taste and remaining sauce. Mix ingredients by hand until just blended. 2. Form 1" thick patties and place on a wax paper lined tray. Place tray with patties in refrigerator and allow to chill for 10-15 minutes. Prepare chili according to package directions. Set aside. 4. Place chilled patties on the grill at 350°F for 5 minutes per side, with a quarter turn halfway through for good sear marks. 5. Top burgers with cheese and allow to melt. Burgers are done when internal temperature reaches 165°F.
4. To serve, place a spoonful of chili on each burger and top with jalapeño slices. For another layer of flavor, spread Chipotle mayonnaise on top of the hamburger bun.

Smoked Brisket

Cooking Time: 10 Hrs

Ingredients:

- 10 ½ lb. beef brisket
- ½ C. paprika
- ¼ C. packed light brown sugar
- 3 Tbsp. salt
- 3 Tbsp. coarse black pepper
- 3 Tbsp. Chili powder
- Apple juice
- Water

Directions:

1. Using a sharp knife, trim the fat from the brisket leaving an even, thin layer on the top. 2. In a medium bowl, combine paprika, light brown sugar, Chili powder, salt and pepper and mix well to make rub seasoning. Using your hands, or a shaker, generously apply rub all over. 3. Wrap the brisket in plastic wrap and refrigerate for at least 12 hours. 4. When setting up the grill, add wood chips/chunks to charcoal and add Smokin' Stone with an aluminum pan on top. Pour apple juice and water into pan, about halfway full. Place a temperature probe at grate level and heat grill to 220°F. 5. Place brisket on grates, fat side up, and allow to smoke for 5 hours. After 5 hours, wrap brisket in butcher paper and return to grill at 220°F. Brisket is done when internal temperature reaches 195°F. Allow brisket to rest for 1 hour.
2. Slice, serve and enjoy!

Spring Tomahawk Steak And Vegetables

Cooking Time: 20 Min

Ingredients:

- 20 oz. Tomahawk steak
- Mixed variety radishes, carrots, turnips, roughly chopped
- ¼ C. melted butter
- 2 oz. basil
- 2 oz. parsley, chopped
- 2 oz. salt
- 2 oz. pepper
- 2 oz. garlic
- 2 oz. smoked paprika
- 2 oz. ground rosemary
- 2 oz. Black and Bleu seasoning (optional)
- Salt and pepper, to taste

Directions:

1. Set grill temp to 350°F.
2. Add mixed variety of chopped radishes, carrots, and turnips to hot cast iron skillet or wok with butter.
3. Add salt and pepper to taste on vegetables.
4. Mix salt, pepper, garlic, smoked paprika, and ground rosemary in a bowl (or use Black & Bleu seasoning).
5. Rub seasoning mix onto both sides of the steak.
6. Add steak to grill and cook 5-8 minutes per side.
7. Add fresh basil and chopped parsley to vegetables.
8. Remove steak when internal temp reaches 145°F for medium rare.

Inch-thick Onion Char-burgers

Cooking Time: 15 Min

Ingredients:

- Angus Ground Beef 85% Lean - 1.5 lbs
- White Bread with Crust Removed - 2 slices
- Milk - 1/4 cup
- Kosher Salt - 1 tsp
- Coarse Ground Pepper - 1/2 tsp
- 1 Clove Garlic - Minced
- Half Large Sweet Onion - Chopped
- Paprika - 1/2 tsp
- Parsley - 1/2 tsp
- Garlic Powder - 1/2 tsp
- Cumin - 1 tsp
- Chili Powder - 1 tsp
- Melted and Cooled Bacon Grease - 3 to 4 Tbsp
- Vegetable Shortening - 1 tsp

Directions:

1. If you have bacon grease on hand, melt 3-4 tbsp in a skillet and set aside to let cool slightly. If you do not have bacon grease, fry 6-8 slices of bacon and spoon 3-4 tbsp aside to let cool slightly.
2. Next you'll want to prep your bread paste. Take the 2 slices of uncrusted white bread and break into small 1/2" pieces and place into small bowl. Add milk and let sit for 5 minutes. Mash down with fork until a paste forms. Set aside.
3. Place ground beef into large mixing bowl. Add salt, pepper, paprika, cumin, parsley, chili powder, garlic powder, minced garlic, chopped fresh onion, bread paste, and slightly cooled bacon grease.
4. Use gloved hands to mix all ingredients evenly into the ground beef. Divide into 4 even portions and form into balls. Flatten each ball to form

inch-thick patties. Make center of patties thinner because it will rise as it cooks.

5. Add one fully lit chimney of coals to your favorite Char-Griller charcoal grill. This is a direct, high-heat cook.

6. Place 12" cast-iron skillet on grill grates and close lid. Allow 5-10 minutes to allow skillet to get nice and hot. Add vegetable shortening to ensure a non-stick sear.

7. Place patties in skillet. Sear 1 minute per side.

8. Remove skillet and carefully place patties on AKORN grates directly over coals. Grill 8-11 minutes flipping once.

9. For best results, monitor temp with instant thermometer. For medium-well, pull burgers off the grill at 150° F.

10. Let rest 5-10 minutes.

11. (Optional) While burgers rest, place 12" cast-iron skillet back on grill and fry your eggs with lid closed. Make sure not to over cook, you want a firm egg, but a "drippy" yolk on the inside. Sunny side up.

12. Add burger patty to your bun, top with egg, and your favorite toppings and get ready for one of the juiciest, thickest, and most flavorful burgers you've ever had!

Smoked Prime Rib

Cooking Time: 8 Hrs

Ingredients:

- 15 lb. Prime Rib
- 2 oz. ground pepper
- 4 oz. coarse salt
- 2 oz. smoked paprika

Directions:

1. Mix salt, pepper, and paprika.
2. Cover rib side of prime rib in seasoning.
3. Flip and season the fat cap side of the prime rib.
4. Pre-heat smoker to 225°F.
5. Add prime rib directly to grates, fat cap up.
6. Smoke prime rib at 40 minutes per pound (About 8 hrs for a 15 lb. prime rib). Remove when internal temp reaches 135°F.
7. Let rest for 30 minutes, then slice, serve and enjoy!

Flavor Pro™ Reverse Seared Steak

Cooking Time: Varies Min

Ingredients:

- 4 Ribeyes
- Salt
- Char-Griller Steak Seasoning
- Compound Butter of Choice

Directions:

1. Set up the Flavor Pro for Indirect cooking
2. Add 20 to 25 charcoal briquettes to one side of the flavor drawer
3. Ignite charcoal with gas burners set to medium high
4. Once charcoal is lit, turn off gas burners and allow to fully ash over
5. Prepare the steak by salting and seasoning both sides with Char-Griller steak Rub
6. Add wood chips or chunks to charcoal
7. Show what has been soaked
8. Adjust smoke stacks until temperature is 250 degrees
9. Add steaks to side away from the coals
10. Cook steaks until they reach 115 degrees.
11. Remove steaks from grill and let rest for 5 minutes while you preheat the grill for direct high heat with the gas burners.
12. Sear steaks until internal temperature is 125. Remove from grill and let rest for 5 minutes.

Breakfast Burritos On The Flat Iron

Ingredients:

- Pack of 8 Breakfast Sausage Circles
- Pack of Shredded Cheese
- Burrito Tortillas (Large)
- Pack of Thick-Cut Bacon
- Dozen Eggs
- Package of Diced Frozen Hash Browns

Directions:

1. Perfect for taking on the go or preparing for the family to add some pizzazz into your mornings, these Breakfast Burritos are easy to assemble and allow you to choose toppings to make it your own.
2. Start with the hash browns on high-med/high heat with some oil. Keep an eye on them. Throw on the sausage and bacon. Cut up the sausage for the burritos. Once everything is cooked, move off to the side Warm-up a burrito to make easier to fold Ladle some eggs on to the griddle Add cheese and other toppings Remove burrito wrap Fold the egg into an omelet place on burrito wrap and fold Enjoy!

Pastrami Swiss Burger

Cooking Time: 40 Min

Ingredients:

- 2 lbs. ground beef
- ½ lb. Pastrami, sliced
- 2 eggs, beaten
- Steak BBQ rub
- 1 C. beef all-purpose sauce
- Swiss cheese, sliced
- Hamburger buns
- Condiments of choice

Directions:

1. Place ground beef in large bowl, add eggs and season with Steak BBQ rub, or your favorite rub, to taste and sauce. Mix ingredients by hand until just blended.
2. Form 1" thick patties and place on a wax paper lined tray. Place tray with patties in refrigerator and allow to chill for 10-15 minutes.
3. Place chilled patties on the grill at 350°F for 5 minutes per side, with a quarter turn halfway through for good sear marks.
4. Bush burgers with more sauce, if desired and top with sliced pastrami and cheese. Allow cheese to melt, about 1-2 minutes. Burgers are done when internal temperature reaches 165°F for medium-rare.

Dry Aged Rib Roast

Cooking Time: 1.5 Hrs

Ingredients:

- 6-8 lb. dry aged rib roast
- ½ C. melted butter
- 4 sprigs of parsley
- 4 sprigs of basil
- 4 sprigs of rosemary
- Kosher salt
- Black pepper
- Paprika
- Garlic

Directions:

1. Finely chop parsley, basil, and rosemary, and mix with melted butter
2. Place rib roast on grill at 350°F over indirect heat and grill for approximately 45 minutes
3. Brush roast with buttered herbs
4. Continue to cook over indirect heat for additional 45 minutes or until internal temp reaches 145°F

Double Stack Cheeseburger

Cooking Time: 15 Min

Ingredients:

- 1 lb. ground beef
- Beef/steak all-purpose sauce
- Steak BBQ rub
- 1 sweet onion, sliced
- 1 tomato, sliced
- 2 slices cheddar or pepper jack cheese
- Hamburger buns
- Condiments of choice

Directions:

1. Place ground beef in large bowl and season to taste with Steak BBQ rub or your favorite rub, and sauce. Mix by hand until just blended. 2. Form 1" thick patties and place on a wax paper lined tray. Place tray with patties in refrigerator and allow to chill for 10-15 minutes. 3. Place the onion slices on the grill at 400°F for 5-7 minutes, flipping halfway through, until tender. 4. Place chilled patties on the grill at 400°F for 3 minutes per side, with a quarter turn halfway through for good sear marks. 5. Top burgers with grilled onions and cheese. Allow cheese to melt and stack one burger on top of the other. Burgers are done when internal temperature reaches 165°F.
2. To serve, add more grilled onions and cheese if desired, top with condiments of choice and enjoy!

London Broil N' Veggie Skewers

Ingredients:

- 2 Pounds London Broil cut into cubes.
- 2 Ounces of Char-Griller Steak
- 1 Ounce Soy Sauce
- 2 Ounces of Honey Mustard.
- 2 Ounces of White Wine Vinegar.
- 2/3 Cup of Extra Virgin Olive Oil
- 1 Ounce Sazón
- 1 Ounce of Fresh Cilantro (Chopped)
- 1 White Onion (Cut into Squares)
- 1 Yellow Pepper (Cut Into Squares)
- 12-15 Baby Bella Mushrooms (Remove Stem)
- 1 Red Pepper (Cut Into Squares)

Directions:

1. Marinade prep.
2. Using a large bowl mix olive oil, cilantro, sazón, steak rub, white wine vinegar, honey mustard & soy sauce. Mix thoroughly.
3. Then add the London Broil meat to the mixture. Mix thoroughly.
4. Allow to rest for 2-24 hours.
5. Skewer prep
6. Add veggies and meat to long metal or bamboo skewers.
7. Tip: I used long metal skewers, the metal skewers helps cook the meat inside quicker due to the heat transferring from the metal. Bamboo skewers are always a good option but tend to burn on the tips and you also have to remember to soak them prior to prepping/cooking them.
8. Preheat your smoker/grill to 340°-350°: allow the grill/smoker to thoroughly warm.
9. Add skewers to the grill and cook for 15 minutes: turn skewers periodically.
10. baste with warmed mixture of olive oil, cilantro, sazón, steak rub, white wine vinegar, honey mustard & soy sauce.
11. Remove after 15 minutes or desired internal temperature and enjoy.

Smoked Beef Chili

Cooking Time: 4 Hrs

Ingredients:

- Chuck Roast - 2 Lbs
- 1 Tbsp Kosher Salt (for beef)
- 1 Tbsp Coarse Black Pepper (for beef)
- 1 tsp Garlic Powder (for beef)
- 1 Tbsp Olive Oil (for beef)
- 3 Tbsp Vegetable Oil
- 1 Large Yellow Onion (Diced)
- 6 Garlic Cloves (Minced)
- 1/4 Cup Chili Powder
- 1 Tbsp Ground Cumin
- 1 (28 oz) Can Diced Tomatoes
- 1 (14 oz) Can Tomato Sauce
- 2 (15 oz) Cans Red Kidney Beans (Rinsed)
- Salt and Pepper to Taste
- Fritos, Cheddar Cheese, Cilantro (Toppings)

Directions:

1. Heat your Char-Griller to a temperature of 275 F. Rub the chuck roast with olive oil and season with the mixture of salt, pepper, and garlic powder. Place chuck roast in the Char-Griller away from the fire.
2. When the chuck roast has reached an internal temp of 165 F pull from the grill and let rest. After 10 minutes cut the chuck roast into cubes.
3. Heat the vegetable oil in a large pan and add onions, season with salt/pepper to taste. Cook until onions have softened.
4. Add minced garlic, chili powder, and cumin to the onions and stir until fragrant. Add the cubed chuck roast and stir until coated with the chili mixture.
5. Transfer the chili mixture into a Dutch oven and add the diced tomatoes, tomato sauce, and beans. Stir well to combine.
6. Place Dutch oven back on grill and continue to cook at a temperature of 275 F. Stir occasionally.
7. When chili has melded, and the beef is fork tender it is ready to serve. Serve with your favorite chili toppers and enjoy!

OTHER FAVORITE RECIPES

Grilled Blue Cheese Wings

Ingredients:

- Fresh Chicken Wing Portions
- 1 Bottle Blue Cheese Dressing
- Salt & Pepper to taste
- 1 Cup Hot Sauce
- 2 Tbsp Butter

Directions:

1. Marinate the chicken wings overnight in the blue cheese dressing.
2. Grill until charred and crispy, and temperature reads at least 165 degrees Fahrenheit.
3. Season with salt and pepper to taste.
4. Melt the butter into the hot sauce, and serve along with the chicken as dip on the side.

2-burner Flat Iron Simple Lo Mein

Cooking Time: 10 Min

Ingredients:

- 1 package of Lo Mein Noodles
- 1 Tbsp of Extra Virgin Olive Oil
- 1 Cup of White or Button Mushrooms (Sliced)
- 2 Tbsp of Minced Garlic
- 4 Cups of Spinach (or another vegetable of your choice)
- 1 Red Pepper (Thinly Sliced)
- 1 Carrot (Shredded)
- 1/2 Cop of Snow Peas
- 2 Tbsp of Soy Sauce
- 2 Tsp of Honey
- 1/2 Tsp of Ground Ginger
- 1 Tsp of Sesame Oil
- 1/2 Tsp of Sriracha or Chili Sauce

Directions:

1. Bring the flavors of your favorite takeout home to your backyard. This simple Lo Mein recipe makes it easy to incorporate your favorite veggies, tailoring it to your liking, while still delivering on explosive flavors. Serve it as a main dinner dish or with a side of your favorite chicken or beef.
2. Cook Lo Mein noodles according to package instructions. Drain and set aside. In a small bowl, combine soy sauce, honey, ginger, sesame oil and sriracha/chili sauce. Mix thoroughly and set to the side. Heat the Flat Iron to medium-high heat. Add oil to the cooktop then add garlic, mushrooms, red pepper, carrot and snow peas. Cook for 3-4 minutes until tender then add spinach and cook until wilted. Pour the soy sauce mixture over vegetables and mix thoroughly. Add Lo Mein noodles then mix thoroughly, ensuring all the noodles become coated and browned. Cook for 2-3 minutes before removing from the cooktop. Serve immediately. Enjoy!

Alabama White Sauce

Cooking Time: 3 Min

Ingredients:

- 2 Cups Mayonnaise
- 1/3 Cup Horseradish
- 2 Tsp Dijon Mustard
- 1/3 Cup Apple Cider Vinegar
- 2 Tbsp Lemon Juice
- 1/4 Tsp Minced Garlic
- 1 Tsp Sea Salt

- 1 Tsp Black Pepper
- 1/2 Tsp Cayenne Pepper
- 1/2 Tsp Oregano Flakes
- 1/2 Tsp Garlic Powder

Directions:

1. Alabama White Sauce is a creamy, tangy, with just a pinch of heat.
2. Combine all the ingredients together in a medium bowl. Whisk until the mixture is creamy. Store in an airtight container and refrigerate until ready to use.

Fresh Summer Corn Avocado Tomato Salad

Cooking Time: 10 Min

Ingredients:

- 2 Cups Cooked Corn (Grilled Is Preferred)
- 2 Avocados Cut Into Small Cubes
- 2 Cherry Tomatoes
- 1/3 Cup Of Chopped Red Onion
- 2 Tbsp Of Extra Virgin Olive Oil
- 1/2 Tsp Of Sea Salt
- 1/2 Tsp Of Black Pepper
- 1 Tbsp Of Lime Juice
- 1/4 Cup Of Cilantro

Directions:

1. Combine the primary salad ingredients: corn, avocado, tomatoes, and red onion in a large bowl. In a small bowl, combine the dressing ingredients: olive oil, sea salt, black pepper, lime juice, and cilantro until they are thoroughly mixed. Pour the dressing over the salad and mix thoroughly. Chill the salad for at least an hour before serving.

Char Grilled Wings

Cooking Time: 20 Min

Ingredients:

- Chicken Wings - 2 to 4 Pounds
- Hot Sauce - 1/2 Cup
- Melted Butter - 1/4 Cup
- Salt - 1 Tablespoon
- Hot Sauce (for Sauce) - 1/2 Cup
- Minced Garlic (for Sauce) - 2 Cloves
- Cayenne - 1 Teaspoon

Directions:

1. If you're like my family, you're counting down the days to football season. That means tailgates at the stadium, or in your own backyard, and if you've got the cute transportable AKORN Jr, Grilled Wings are absolutely in your tailgating future.
2. I do my wings a little differently, I like to soak them in plain old cayenne vinegar hot sauce for 48 hours before I grill them. This is 100% optional, but I'm telling you- the flavor profile is unreal. Add a few hunks of Applewood to your charcoal while grilling these for a flavor explosion. Pro Tip: Baste your wings in the sauce at the very end to keep them from burning. Since they marinated in the hot sauce for hours, the flavor is packed in. Let's dig in.
3. After rinsing and drying your wings, toss in hot sauce, avocado oil, and salt. Marinate for 24-48 hours.
4. When you're ready to grill, add a few chunks of Applewood to your charcoal, and get the grill nice and hot. Oil your grates and spread the wings out evenly. Grill on each side for 8 minutes, until crispy and golden brown.
5. While the wings finish cooking, brush the buffalo sauce over each side, and turn 1-2 more times to allow the sauce to caramelize. Dip them in your favorite ranch or blue cheese, and enjoy!

Smoked Mac 'n Cheese

Cooking Time: 25-30 Min

Ingredients:

- 1 lb. elbow macaroni
- 3 C. milk
- 6 Tbsp. unsalted butter
- ½ C. all-purpose flour
- 2 C. smoked Gouda cheese, grated
- 1 C. shredded Cheddar, grated
- 1½ C. panko breadcrumbs
- ½ Tsp. black pepper
- 1 Tsp. garlic powder
- ½ Tsp. onion powder
- ½ Tsp. mustard powder
- Kosher salt, to taste

Directions:

1. Add pasta to a large pot of boiling salted water and cook according to package directions, 6-8 minutes. Drain well.
2. Meanwhile, heat the milk in a small saucepan until hot, being careful not to boil it. Whisk together 6 Tbsp. butter and flour in a large pot. Gradually add hot milk and cook for 1-2 minutes, stirring continuously, until thickened and smooth.
3. Remove from heat and add cheese, salt, to taste, and pepper, garlic powder, onion powder and mustard powder. Add cooked macaroni and stir well. Spoon mixture into cast iron pan.
4. Stir in breadcrumbs and sprinkle on top. Place pan on the grill at 350°F with a Smokin' Stone under the grates and bake for 25-30 minutes, or until the sauce is bubbly and the macaroni is lightly browned on top.

Mediterranean Veggie Burgers With Vegan Feta Dip

Ingredients:

- 1 1/2 Cups Brown Rice (Cooked)
- 1 1/2 Cups Sweet Potato (Steamed Or Roasted)
- 1 Egg
- 2 Cloves Garlic
- 3-4 Pepperoncini Peppers (Drained)
- 1/4 Cup Parsley (Fresh)
- 6 Buns
- 2 Tbsp Olive Oil
- Salt & Pepper To Taste
- Lettuce, Tomato, And Onion For Toppings
- 1/2 Cup Vegan Mayo, Or Vegan Yogurt
- 2 Tbsp Parsley (Chopped)
- 2 Pepperoncini Peppers (Chopped)
- 1 Clove Garlic (Minced)
- 1 Tbsp Lemon Zest
- 1 Tbsp Olive Oil
- Salt & Pepper To Taste

Directions:

1. In a food processor, combine brown rice, sweet potato, egg, garlic, pepperoncini peppers,parsley, salt and pepper, and pulse until well combined. You can also mash these ingredients with a fork if you prefer a chunkier texture, just dice the garlic, parsley, and peppers first.
2. Wet hands slightly, and form mixture into six evenly shaped patties. Let chill in the fridge or freezer for 10 minutes, until burgers have a chance to firm up a bit.
3. Combine ingredients(12-19) for Feta Dip and set aside. Pro Tip: dip is even better the next day

after the flavors marry, if you have time to make it the day before!

4. Preheat Flat-Iron Gas Griddle to medium heat, and drizzle olive oil over the surface, using a towel and tongs to spread it across the griddle. Once it's been heating up for a few minutes, add burgers and buns to the grill. Let buns toast for 1 minute, then remove. Let burgers cook for 5 minutes on the first side, flip, then finish cooking for 5 more minutes.

5. Remove burgers from grill and begin assembling, piling L,T,O, and a burger on the toasted buns, finishing with a dollop of feta dip! Enjoy while warm! These burgers can keep in the fridge for 5 days, or frozen for up to three months.

Grilled Corn

Cooking Time: 10 Min

Ingredients:

- 6 ears of corn, shucked
- 1/2 Cup of Butter
- Kosher Salt
- Optional: Char-Griller Garlic & Herb Rub

Directions:

1. Heat grill to high heat. Add corn to the grates, turning often until they develop a char, 10-15 minutes. Remove corn from the grill and spread butter all over, then season to taste with salt. Serve hot or warm. Enjoy!

Fabulous Buttermilk Pancakes

Cooking Time: 4 Min

Ingredients:

- 2 Cups All Purpose Flour
- 1 Tsp Baking Soda
- 1 Tsp Salt
- 1 Tablespoon Sugar
- 1 Egg
- 3 Cups Buttermilk

Directions:

1. Preheat part of your griddle to 375°-400° Mix well all the dry and ingredients Mix the buttermilk into the dry ingredients, it's ok if lumpy. In a separate bowl, crack the egg and whisk it incorporating air into the egg until it is light and bubbly. Eggs that are not straight out of the refrigerator will whip up easier. Add the egg to the other ingredients and mix, JUST to incorporate. DO NOT OVERMIX Grease the area of the griddle for pancakes with vegetable oil Drop approximately 1/2 cup plus a little bit more of the batter onto the hot griddle and let it spread out. Cook until the bottom side is golden brown. Flip pancake and lightly brown. Serve with butter and warm maple syrup. Enjoy these light fluffy pancakes

Serrano Beer Cheese

Cooking Time: 20 Min

Ingredients:

- Beer (your favorite) - 1.75 Cups
- Serrano Peppers - 5
- Shredded White Cheddar Cheese - 3 Cups
- Cream Cheese - 8 oz.
- Char-Griller Steak Seasoning - 1 Tbsp
- Cilantro - For Garnish

Directions:

1. Pre-heat grill to at least 350 degrees Fahrenheit
2. Roast serrano peppers over direct heat until skin blisters
3. Remove peppers and place in sandwich bag
4. Remove skins from peppers and de seed all but one

5. Chop peppers into small pieces
6. Add beer and peppers to cast iron skillet
7. Allow to simmer for 5 minutes
8. Add cream cheese and whisk until smooth
9. Add shredded cheese and whisk until melted completely
10. Sprinkle seasoning over the cheese and stir to combine
11. Garnish with cilantro
12. Enjoy with chips, soft pretzels or spoon it over a burger

Grilled Cilantro Garlic Parmesan Chicken Wings

Cooking Time: 30 Min

Ingredients:

- Room Temperature Water - 8 Cups
- Course Kosher Salt - 1/3 Cup
- Sugar - 1 Tablespoon
- Chicken Wings with Tips Removed, Drumettes and Flats Separated - 3 to 4 Pounds
- Oil for Grilling - 1 Tablespoon
- Unsalted Butter - 1/2 Cup
- Minced Garlic Cloves - 4
- Smoked Paprika - 1 Teaspoon
- Course Kosher Salt - 1 Teaspoon
- Black Pepper - 1/4 Teaspoon
- Grated Parmesan Cheese - 1/4 Cup
- Parmesan Cheese for Garnish - 2 Tablespoons

Directions:

1. These wings are quick-brined for 30 minutes in a simple solution of water, salt and sugar to achieve that juicy tender inside and crispy crunchy outside. They're tossed in a generous mixture of melted butter infused with garlic, parmesan, smoked paprika and salt.
2. Top the wings with some freshly chopped cilantro to add some bright Mexican-inspired flavors and enjoy!
3. Make a quick brine: In a large bowl, add water, coarse kosher salt and sugar. Stir together until the sugar and salt have completely dissolved. Add the chicken wings, cover the bowl with plastic wrap and refrigerate for 30 minutes.
4. Prepare wings: Remove the chicken wings from the brine and pat completely dry with paper towels. Place in a large mixing bowl, add in 1 tablespoon oil for grilling and toss together to coat.
5. Prepare the grill: Preheat grill to medium-high heat (about 400°F-450°F). Brush the preheated grill grate with cooking oil to prevent sticking by wiping it down with a folded paper towel that has been soaked in vegetable oil.
6. Grill the wings: Grill the chicken wings with the lid closed for about 8 minutes per side, rearranging them on the grill accordingly if you notice that some wings are cooking faster than others. Grilled wings are ready when the meat is no longer pink at the bone and the temperature in the thickest part registers at least 165°F. Remove from the grill and transfer to a large bowl.
7. Make the wing sauce: Heat a small pot or saucepan over medium heat. Add the butter and melt. Add the garlic and saute until fragrant, about 30 seconds. Add the smoked paprika, 2 tablespoons grated Parmesan cheese, black pepper and salt. Stir together to combine and remove from heat. 6. Coat the wings: Pour half of the garlic Parmesan wing sauce onto the grilled wings. Add the remaining 2 tablespoons grated Parmesan cheese and toss with the wings to combine. Pour the other half of the sauce in a

small bowl or ramekin to serve as a dipping sauce if desired.

8. Serve: Top the wings with chopped cilantro and shredded Parmesan cheese. Serve with the reserved garlic Parmesan sauce and enjoy.

Fresh Chili Lime Watermelon Fries

Cooking Time: 5 Min

Ingredients:

- 1 Seedless Watermelon
- 2 Tsp of Tajin Chili Lime Seasoning
- 1 Tsp of Sea Salt
- 1 Cup Greek Yogurt
- 1/2 Fresh Squeezed Lime
- 1/2 Tsp of Chili Powder
- 1 Tbsp Honey

Directions:

1. Slice the watermelon into long, "french fry" formation. Combine the sea salt, and chili lime seasoning in a large bowl. In a separate bowl, combine yogurt, lime juice, chili powder, and honey. Mix thoroughly. Serve the yogurt mixture alongside the watermelon for easy dipping.

Grillinguy's Best Veggie Burger

Cooking Time: 10 Min

Ingredients:

- 1 Tbsp Olive Oil
- 1/2 Of a Sweet Onion (Minced)
- 3 Garlic Cloves (Minced)
- 1 Cup Cooked Quinoa
- 2 Cups Walnuts
- 1 15 Oz Can Of Pinto Beans
- 1/4 Cup Italian Seasoning
- 1/3 Cup Breadcrumbs
- 1 Tbsp Soy Sauce
- 1 Tsp Chili Powder
- 1 Tsp Cumin
- 1 Tsp Salt

Directions:

1. In a skillet over medium heat, add olive oil. Add onion and sauté until soften Add garlic and sauté for 30 seconds Set aside in a large bowl In food processor, add walnuts and pulse until crumb-like consistency. Add to bowl with onions Mash pintos and add to bowl Add in quinoa, soy sauce, Italian seasoning, chili powder, cumin, bread crumbs and salt Form into patties and place on baking sheet lined with parchment paper and refrigerate for an hour When ready to cook, preheat grill to medium high heat. Add patties and cook until brown on both sides Layer your bun with favorite toppings and enjoy

Flat Iron Cereal French Toast

Cooking Time: 15 Min

Ingredients:

- 2 Cup of Crushed Cereal (Your Favorite Kind)
- 12 Slices of Thick Sliced Bread
- 4 Eggs
- 1/2 Cup Brown Sugar
- 1/2 Cup Heavy Cream
- 1 Cup Whole Milk
- 1 Tbsp Cinnamon
- 1 Tbsp Vanilla
- Pinch of Salt
- 1/4 Butter

Directions:

1. Heat flat iron with one side burner on low and others right between low and medium
2. Toast bread on griddle for a few minutes on each side to dry out slightly and remove promptly

3. Whisk together sugar, cinnamon, and eggs until creamy and mixed thoroughly (this is the secret to not having an eggy ring on your French toast)
4. Add cream, milk, vanilla, and salt to egg mixture and whisk thoroughly
5. Dip a slice of bread into the mixture and flip to coat
6. Dip the slice of bread into the crushed cereal and turn to coat
7. Place butter on griddle and allow to melt, spread evenly across griddle
8. Place each slice of French toast on griddle and allow to toast for 4-5 minutes per side
9. When toasted and cooked through, place slices of bread on the low heat side of the griddle until the remainder is finished

Easter Sunday Coleslaw For Pulled Pork Sandwiches

Cooking Time: 5 Min

Ingredients:

- Shredded Cabbage Mix - 2 Cups
- Kosher Salt - 1 1/2 tsp
- Sour Cream - 1/4 Cup
- Mayonnaise - 2 Tbs
- Apple Cider Vinegar - 1 Tbs
- Coarse Black Pepper - 2 tsp
- Dry Mustard Powder - 1 1/2 tsp

Directions:

1. During the cook time of the pork is when I put my coleslaw together.
2. Pour your cabbage into a large bowl and make sure that you try to dab away any extra water it may have on it.
3. In a small bowl combine all your coleslaw ingredients and stir thoroughly.
4. Transfer the mixture into the bowl with the cabbage and stir until it is well coated.
5. Store in refrigerator until it is time to serve.
6. Put slaw on top of pulled pork, top with a bun, and enjoy!

Butternut Squash Soup

Cooking Time: 45-50 Min

Ingredients:

- 1 large butternut squash, halved and seeded
- ½ C. chopped shallot
- 1 Tsp. salt
- 4 garlic cloves, minced
- 1 Tsp. maple syrup
- ⅛ Tsp. ground nutmeg
- Freshly ground black pepper, to taste
- 3-4 C. vegetable broth
- 1-2 Tbsp. butter
- 1-2 Tbsp. heavy whipping cream
- Olive oil

Directions:

1. Pre-heat the grill to 425°F. Rub 1 Tsp. of olive oil over the inside of both halves of the squash and sprinkle with salt and pepper. Wrap each half in foil, adding a ½ C. water to each. 2. Place on the grill and bake for 45-50 minutes, until squash is tender and completely cooked through. Remove from grill and allow to cool for 10 minutes. Unwrap, and use a large spoon to scoop the flesh into a bowl, discarding the skin. 3. In a large soup pot over medium heat, add olive oil and chopped shallot and sauté until the shallot has softened, 3-4 minutes. Add garlic and cook until fragrant, about 1 minute, stirring frequently. 4. Transfer the cooked shallot and garlic to a blender. Add the squash, maple syrup, nutmeg and freshly ground black pepper, to taste. Slowly

add vegetable broth and blend until creamy. 5. Add 1- 2 Tbsp. heavy whipping cream to taste, and blend well. Taste and blend in more salt and pepper, if needed.

2. Serve immediately. Let leftover soup cool completely and refrigerate for up to 4 days or freeze for up to 3 months.

Bbq Fiends Oktoberfest Beer Brats

Cooking Time: 25 Min

Ingredients:

- 5 Bratwurst
- 1 - 12 oz Can or Bottle of Oktoberfest Beer
- 1/2 Large White Onion - Sliced
- 5 Bratwurst Buns
- 1/2 Can or Jar of Sauerkraut
- Whole Grain Brown Mustard
- Kosher Salt
- Coarse Black Pepper

Directions:

1. Pre-heat the grill to 375 F and place a lightly oiled large skillet on the grill
2. Sauté the sliced onions in the oil and add salt and pepper to taste. Once the onions are tender add the can of beer into the skillet.
3. Bring the beer to a boil and add the bratwurst to the skillet.
4. Remove the bratwurst once the beer as almost reduced completely and set the bratwurst directly on the grill. Rotate on both sides for 2-3 minutes or until internal temp is at 160 F.
5. Serve the bratwurst in a bun with the beer onions, sauerkraut, and mustard as toppings. Enjoy!

Grilled Garlic Bread

Cooking Time: 3-5 Min

Ingredients:

- 1 Loaf of French bread
- 1 Cup Of Salted Butter(Soft)
- 5 Tbsp Of Extra Virgin Olive Oil
- 1 1/2 Tbsp Of Minced Garlic
- 2 Tsp Of Parsley
- 2- 3 Tbsp Char-Griller "Garlic & Herb" Rub

Directions:

1. Preheat your grill to medium heat. Combine all ingredients aside from bread into a bowl and whip together. You should have a whipped, buttery consistency. Split the bread in half lengthwise before cutting in half or simply cut it into slices. Spread the mixture onto the face of the bread. Lightly brush some of the mixture onto the sides and bottom as well. Place your bread on the grill and cook for 3-5 minutes or until desired crispness or brownness before flipping over. Remove from the grill and if there are burnt minced garlic pieces, feel free to brush them off. Sprinkle with parsley and cut to desired serving sizes. Serve warm, enjoy!

Sweet And Tangy Apple Coleslaw

Cooking Time: 10 Min

Ingredients:

- 3 Cups Chopped Cabbage
- 1 Cup Grated Carrots
- 1/4 Cup Of Thinly Sliced Red Bell Peppers
- 1/4 Cup Of Thinly Sliced Green Bell Peppers
- 1 Cup Of Green Onions (Finely Chopped)
- 1/2 Cup Of Mayonnaise
- 1 Tbsp Fresh Lemon Juice
- 1/4 Cup Brown Sugar

- 1 Unpeeled Red Apple (Cored & Chopped)

Directions:

1. In a large bowl, combine cabbage, red and green apples, carrots, and green onions. In a small bowl, combine mayonnaise, lemon juice, and brown sugar. Pour the dressing over the salad. And mix thoroughly. For best results, chill for at least one hour before serving.

Keto Grilled Brie

Cooking Time: 10 Min

Ingredients:

- Wheel of Brie- 1
- Chopped Pecans
- Chopped Strawberries
- Minced Fresh Basil
- Sugar Free Honey
- Balsamic Vinegar

Directions:

1. Grill a wheel of brie over medium high heat for 5 minutes per side, or until nice and soft with grill marks.
2. Meanwhile, toast chopped pecans in a mini cast iron over the same medium high grill heat.
3. Top with chopped strawberries, minced fresh basil, the warm pecans, and a glaze made from: one part sugar free honey, one part balsamic vinegar

Flat Iron French Toast

Cooking Time: 7 To 9 Min

Ingredients:

- 8 Slices Low-Carb Brioche Bread
- 6 Eggs
- 2 Tbsp Heavy Whipping Cream
- 1 tsp Cinnamon
- 1 tsp Sweetener

Directions:

1. Preheat Flat Iron to medium high.
2. Combine eggs, whipping cream, cinnamon, and sweetener (Shenna uses Monkfruit) and whisk thoroughly.
3. Dip bread slices into mixture and ensure they are fully coated.
4. Places slices on griddle and flip after about 3 to 4 minutes.
5. Flip and add butter on top while the other side cooks.
6. Remove from griddle and serve with fruit, syrup, whipped cream and more!

Gravity 980 Quick N' Fast Grilled Vegetables

Cooking Time: 5 Min

Ingredients:

- 1 Large Zucchini (Sliced)
- 1 Large Summer Squash (Sliced)
- 1 Red Bed Pepper (Sliced)
- 3 Large Portobello Mushrooms (Sliced)
- 1 Red Onion (Sliced)
- Kosher Salt
- Black Pepper
- 1 Tbsp of Garlic Powder
- 1 Tsp of Paprika
- 1 Tbsp of Italian Seasoning (or your choice of herbs)
- 1/2 Cup of Extra Virgin Olive Oil

Directions:

1. Remove the fire shutter from the Gravity 980. Load the hopper and set the temperature to 400°F. In a large bowl, combine all veggies with olive oil and seasonings. Place a grill wok on the

grates and close the grill, allowing it to preheat for 2-3 minutes before adding vegetable mixture. Using a silicone spatula, open the grill and stir vegetables around in the wok, repeating the process until vegetables reach desired doneness. Serve hot or warm. Enjoy!

Dirty Bird Chicken Wings

Cooking Time: 30 Min

Ingredients:

- 12 to 14 Whole Chicken Wings
- Olive Oil
- Char-Griller Creole Seasoning to Taste
- Sazon to Taste
- Adobo to Taste
- Char-Griller Lemon Pepper Rub
- Garlic Powder to Taste

Directions:

1. Rinse Chicken Wings with cold water and pat dry.
2. Trim/remove access fat, skin and hair.
3. Apply coating of olive oil to both sides of the chicken.
4. Add Sazon, Char-Griller Grills Creole, Char-Griller Grills Lemon Pepper and adobo seasonings.
5. Heat up the AKORN Kamado with lump charcoal to 375°
6. Place the chicken wings in the grill.
7. Flip the wings in 15 minutes.
8. Grill the chicken wings until internal 175° and remove.
9. Eat them right off the grill and enjoy!

Smoked Chicken Thighs And Veggies

Cooking Time: 30 Min

Ingredients:

- 4 Chicken Thighs (Skinless)
- 1 Crown Broccoli (Chopped)
- 1 Crown Cauliflower (Chopped)
- Smoked Cherrywood Sea Salt (To Taste)
- Rosy Cheeks Maple Bourbon Rub (To Taste)
- Bold Bayou Cajun (To Taste)

Directions:

1. Remove the skin from the chicken thighs; I start with the loose skin by the knuckle, grab the skin from underneath and pull up.
2. Season both sides of the thighs with sea salt. We use the smoked cherrywood sea salt to begin our layers.
3. Season both sides of the thighs with Rosy Cheeks (we did one in Bold Bayou ~ it's a little more cajun style and spicy). This is called layering your seasonings.
4. As the chicken sweats, chop up your veggies. Add them to a bowl and toss with oil and salt.
5. Heat your grill up to 250° - 275° for a low and slow cook.
6. Add chicken and veggies to the grill; add your smoking chips.
7. After about 10 minutes flip the chicken and veggies; feel free to add more chips if need be.
8. After about another 10 minutes begin to probe your chicken. You're looking for clear juices and a temp of no less than 165°. When you reach that Internal Temp (IT) pull the chicken and let it rest. Pull the veggies when crisp

Flavor Pro Hot And Fast Ribs

Cooking Time: 3 To 4 Hrs

Ingredients:

- 2 Racks of Ribs
- Char-Griller Rib Rub

- 1 Cup Apple Juice
- 1/4 Cup Brown Sugar
- 8 Tbsp Butter
- BBQ Sauce of Choice
- Wood Chips of Choice

Directions:

1. Remove membrane from ribs and season liberally on both sides with Char-Griller Rib Rub.
2. Set up the Flavor Pro for Indirect cooking
3. Add 15 to 20 charcoal briquettes to one side of the flavor drawer
4. Ignite charcoal with gas burners set to medium high
5. Once charcoal is lit, turn off gas burners and allow to fully ash over.
6. Add a handful of soaked wood chips to charcoal.
7. Using a grilling glove, adjust smokestacks until grill is 300 degrees.
8. Place ribs bone side down on the opposite side of the grill as the charcoal and wood and allow to cook for 2 and a half hours at 300 degrees.
9. Remove ribs from grill and place bone side up on a large sheet of tin foil. Fold up the foil to create a well and add ½ apple juice to the ribs.
10. Add 1/8 cup of brown sugar and 4 tablespoons of butter to the top of the ribs.
11. Close foil tightly around ribs and place back on the 300 degree grill for 1 hour and 15 minutes.
12. Add more charcoal if needed.
13. Remove ribs from foil and place back on grill. Brush with your favorite BBQ sauce and cook for an additional 15 minutes.

Grilled Red Onion And Brussel Sprouts Skewers

Cooking Time: 15 Min

Ingredients:

- 1 Lb of Brussel Sprouts
- 1 Large Red Onion
- 1/4 Cup of Extra Virgin Olive Oil
- 1/4 Cup of Balsamic Vinegar
- 1 Tbsp of Garlic (Minced)
- 1 Tsp of Paprika
- 1 Tsp of Garlic Powder
- 1 Tsp of Onion Powder
- 1 Tsp of Celery Salt
- Sea Salt and Pepper to Taste
- Pack of Skewers
- 1/4 Cup of Chopped Bacon (Optional)
- 1/4 Cup of Goat Cheese Crumbled (Optional)

Directions:

1. Preheat the grill to high setting or fire up coals. Cut brussel sprouts into halves and combine in a bowl with olive oil, minced garlic, and all seasonings. Cut onion into thick slices and mix in with brussel sprouts. Add brussel sprouts to skewers in a sequence of brussel sprout half, 2-3 onion slices, brussel sprout half, etc. Place skewers on the grill and turn often until sprouts and onions are fully cooked and tender. This will take between 10-15 minutes. Serve warm. Optionally, remove from skewers and combine in a bowl with bacon and crumbled goat cheese. Serve warm or refrigerate and serve cold.

Griddle Cheesesteaks

Cooking Time: 15 Min

Ingredients:

- 2 Lbs of Shaved Beef Steak
- 2 Tbsp of Extra Virgin Olive Oil
- 2 Cups of Thinly Sliced White Onions
- 1 Cup of Chopped Green Peppers
- 4 Sub Rolls
- 4 Tbsp of Unsalted Butter
- 12 Slices of Provolone Cheese
- Sea Salt and Black Pepper to taste

Directions:

1. Heat the olive oil on medium heat in one zone of Flat Iron. Add onion and green peppers, seasoning with desired amount of sea salt and black pepper. Stir until softened. Remove from heat. Add raw steak to the same zone of the Flat Iron on medium heat. Lightly season with salt and pepper to taste. Using spatulas, shred and stir steak, ensuring all of the steak browns. Add onion and peppers to steak and thoroughly mix together, allowing them to continue to cook together for 2 minutes. At the same time, melt butter in a separate zone on medium heat. Place rolls open and faced down and allow the inside to brown and lightly toast. Set aside. Separate steak into 4 equal piles then add 3 slices of cheese to melt along each pile. Place one toasted sub roll face down on top of each steak pile and use spatula to scoop steak, onion and pepper mixture into the roll. Serve hot, enjoy.

Flat Iron Spinach & Feta Omelette

Cooking Time: 10 Min

Ingredients:

- 2 Large Eggs
- 2 Tsp of Butter
- 1 Cup Spinach (Chopped)
- 1 Tsp of Water or Milk
- 2 Tbsp of Feta Cheese (Crumbled)
- 1/2 Tsp of Salt
- 1/2 Tsp of Pepper
- 1/2 Tsp of Cayenne Pepper
- 1/2 Tsp of Garlic Powder

Directions:

1. Heat the Flat Iron to medium heat. Melt the butter.
2. Add spinach to the griddle and stir until slightly softened.
3. While spinach cooks, in a small bowl, whisk together the eggs, water or milk, and seasonings for 1 minute.
4. Pour the egg mixture over the spinach.
5. Sprinkle feta cheese crumbles evenly over egg.
6. Once the egg begins to set at the bottom, use a spatula to occasionally raise the edges of the omelette so that uncooked egg will run off from the top.
7. Once it is cooked completely through, fold it in half or into thirds.
8. Serve hot.

Flat Iron Lime Chicken And Mango Salsa Quesadillas

Cooking Time: 20 Min

Ingredients:

- 1 Lb of Chicken Breast, Shredded or Sliced into thin Strips or Bite sized pieces
- 1 Tsp of Salt
- 1 Tsp of Pepper
- 1 Tsp of Garlic Powder
- 1 Tsp of Cumin

- 1 Tsp of Parsley
- 1/2 Tsp of Paprika
- 1/2 Tsp of Cayenne Pepper
- 1 1/2 Tbsp of Fresh Lime Juice
- 1 1/2 Tbsp of Extra Virgin Olive Oil
- 2 Mangoes, Diced (If not ripe/sweet enough, may add small drizzle of Honey)
- 1 Red Pepper (Diced)
- 1/4 Cup of Cilantro (Chopped)
- 1 Tsp of Fresh Lime Juice
- 3 Cups of Pepper Jack, Monterrey Jack, Colby Jack or Mexican Blend Cheese(Your Choice)
- 4 Large Flour Tortillas
- 2 Tbsp of Butter for Pan

Directions:

1. Preheat Flat Iron to Medium Heat.
2. In a large bowl, mix together chicken pieces, desired oil and all seasonings until every piece is coated.
3. Add chicken to griddle and saute 5-7 minutes until cooked through and lightly browned. Add lime juice and cook for another 2-3 minutes. Remove from griddle.
4. In a small bowl, combine ingredients 10-15 for the mango salsa.
5. On a plate or tray, begin to assemble the quesadillas. Sprinkle cheese to fully cover half of a flour tortilla, add seasoned chicken and salsa, top with more cheese and fold.
6. Reheating the griddle to Medium Heat, add 2 Tbsp of butter and allow it to melt down. Place tortillas on top of butter and flip every 2 minutes until cheese is melted and both sides reach desired crispiness.
7. Serve warm.

Smoked Sweet Garlic Chili And Teriyaki Wings

Cooking Time: 30 Min

Ingredients:

- 1 Bag Of Party Wings
- Favorite Wing Rub
- G. Hughes Sugar Free Teriyaki Marinade
- Garlic Chili Paste
- Monk fruit sweetener
- Apple Cider Vinegar

Directions:

1. WINGS
2. Pat wings dry with paper towel and season with favorite wing rub (I like a maple bourbon base rub for chicken). Heat your grill up to 350*, coating the grates with oil while they warm up (for nonstick) Place wings on grill and cook for about 15 mins, flip wings over and cook for about another 15 mins. Chicken is technically done at 165* IT but I like to take my wings to about 175*-180*ish; this gives them a more fall off the bone texture while crisping the skin. Toss wings in Teriyaki or Sweet Garlic Chili sauce
3. SWEET GARLIC CHILI SAUCE
4. Mix ½ bottle of Garlic Chili sauce with ¼ cup of apple cider vinegar and monk fruit sweetener (to taste) in a pan over medium heat. Stir ingredients until everything has combined Pour directly over wings and toss

2-burner Flat Iron Omelet Rounds

Cooking Time: 15 Min

Ingredients:

- 4 Large Eggs
- 4 Tbsp of Milk or Water

- 1/3 Cup of Shredded Cheese
- Salt and Pepper to taste
- Optional Toppings: Diced Onion, Diced Peppers, Diced Mushroom, Chopped Bacon or Sausage

Directions:

1. In a small bowl, whisk together your eggs, milk/water, salt, pepper, and any desired ingredients. Preheat your Flat Iron to medium heat. Gently grease the inside of your egg rings (Optionally, you can use a large outer slice of an onion). Place them on the cooktop and allow them to warm up for 2-3 minutes. Carefully pour your egg mixture into each ring, filling nearly to the top. To thoroughly cook the egg all around, cover with the Char-Griller Basting Dome. Cook for about 10 minutes until eggs are cooked to your liking. Add cheese to the top of each round and cover once more with the Basting Dome. Remove from the Flat Iron. Serve immediately. Enjoy!

Barbecue Chicken Foil Packets

Ingredients:

- Barbecue Sauce of Choice - 3/4 Cup
- Honey - 2 Tbs
- Apple Cider Vinegar - 3 Tbs
- Smoked Paprika - 1 tsp
- Chili Powder - 1/2 tsp
- Olive Oil - 1 to 2 Tbs
- 4 Boneless, Skinless Chicken Breasts
- 1 Zucchini
- 1 Red Bell Pepper
- 1 Red Onion
- Salt and Pepper to Taste
- Fresh Parsley

Directions:

1. Preheat grill to medium-high heat
2. Tear off or cut four large squares of foil
3. Chop the veggies into chunks
4. Place a chicken breast in the middle of each piece of foil
5. Divide vegetables evenly among packets
6. Drizzle chicken and vegetables with oil and season with salt and pepper to taste
7. In a bowl, mix barbecue sauce, honey, vinegar, chili power and paprika
8. Brush sauce on chicken and reserve some for later
9. Place foil packets on the grill for 7 to 8 minutes, then flip and grill for 6 to 8 minutes.
10. Remove from grill, carefully open packets, brush chicken with reserve sauce, top with parsley and serve.

Oktoberfest Skillet

Ingredients:

- 2 White Potatoes
- Olive Oil - 2 Tbsp
- Caraway Seeds - 1/2 Tbsp
- 4 Thick Cut Bacon Slices
- 4 Brats
- Medium Yellow Onion - Diced
- Red Apple - Diced
- 1/3 Red Cabbage - Diced
- Dijon Mustard - 1 Tbsp
- Sauerkraut - 1/2 Cup
- 12 oz German Style Beer
- Fresh Pepper - 1/2 tsp
- Ground Nutmeg - 1/2 tsp
- Fresh Sage - For Garnish, If Desired

Directions:

1. Preheat grill for medium-high indirect cooking.

2. Combine diced potatoes, olive oil, and caraway seeds in a cast iron skillet. Cook over indirect heat for 30 to 45 minutes.
3. Grill bacon and brats over direct heat. 3 minutes per side.
4. Slice bacon and brats and combine with onions, sauerkraut, apple, cabbage, pepper, nutmeg, beer, and potatoes in skillet.
5. Cook over indirect heat for 20 minutes.
6. Serve with pretzels and beer.

Certified Creole Grilled Chicken N' Sausage Filé Gumbo

Cooking Time: 2 To 3 Hrs

Ingredients:

- Whole Chicken - Cut Up
- Kielbasa Sausage - 4 Links
- Accent Seasoning
- Kary's Roux
- Crisco All-Vegetable Oil
- Cajun/Creole Seasoning - To Taste
- Black Pepper
- Olive Oil
- One White Onion - Diced
- 1 Whole Garlic - Diced
- Filé: Pounded or powdered sassafras leaves
- Paprika
- Chicken Flavor Bouillon
- White Rice
- Cornbread

Directions:

1. Generously coat both of sides of the chicken with olive oil: I used Pig Stand BBQ Cajun Garlic Butter.
2. Season chicken to taste on both sides with Cajun/Creole seasoning: I used Queen Bee Cajun seasoning, Paprika, Accent, Black Pepper.
3. Preheat grill to 400° On the charcoal side of the grill.
4. Add chicken to grill and cook chicken only until the pink is out the chicken.
5. Major Key: Don't cook the chicken fully only want to get the pink out. Then add add to Gumbo. Doing this allows the chicken to get flavor from the grill, get tenderized and become soft while in the Gumbo.
6. Preheat large pot on side burner of the grill on high.
7. Add generous portion Crisco All Vegetable Oil to coat the bottom of the pot.
8. Once oil is melted and hot add the diced onion until they become soft then add chopped whole or jarred garlic. This takes about 10 mins.
9. Add water: fill pot with water roughly quarter high to start.
10. Season water with with paprika, accent, black pepper,Filé, Cajun/Creole seasoning, chicken flavor bouillon to taste. Close lid and let simmer.
11. After simmering for roughly 8-10 mins then add roux to taste: I normally make a homemade roux but tried out Kary's Roux for the first time. Then add additional water.
12. Tip: don't over fill with water because the water will rise in Gumbo when the chicken and sausages are added.
13. After the Gumbo has simmered for an additional 10 mins, lower the heat on the side burner to low. Then add the chicken & sausages off the grill to the gumbo.
14. Tip: Be sure to char the sausages, added so much additional flavor to the Gumbo.
15. Then allow the Gumbo to cook on low for 1-2 hours and stir every so often. The chicken & sausages will be extremely tender and juicy.

16. Make white rice on the side burner.
17. Make your favorite cornbread in a cast iron skillet on the gas side of the grill.
18. Serve and enjoy.
19. Tip: sprinkle some additional Filé for some extra tasty flavor.

Smoked Roasted Vegetables

Cooking Time: 15 Min

Ingredients:

- 1 medium onion
- 1 zucchini
- 1 small green bell pepper
- 1 small red bell pepper
- 1 small yellow bell pepper
- Vegetable oil, for brushing
- Salt and pepper, to taste

Directions:

1. Pre-heat grill to 400°F. Rinse all produce and pat dry with paper towel. 2. Slice bell peppers in half and remove stem, core and seeds. Remove outer layers of onion and slice in half. Slice zucchini in half and remove ends. 3. Place vegetables on grill, equally spaced apart and grill for 10-12 minutes, turning occasionally, until vegetables are tender and grill marks develop. Skins of bell peppers should be lightly charred. 4. Lightly brush vegetables with olive oil. Sprinkle with salt and pepper or your favorite seasoning.
2. Slice vegetables into 1" strips when cooled enough to handle and serve. Enjoy!

Caprese Grilled Chicken

Cooking Time: 20 Min

Ingredients:

- 4 Boneless Skinless Whole Chicken Breasts
- 4 Slices of Fresh Mozzarella Cheese
- 6 Slices of Roma Tomato
- 6 Large Basil Leaves
- 2 Tbsp of Unsalted Butter
- 1/4 Cup of Balsamic Vinegar
- 2 Tsp of Salt
- 2 Tsp of Black Pepper
- 1 Tsp of Dried Oregano
- 1 Tsp of Dried Basil
- 1/2 Tsp of Cayenne Pepper
- 1 Tsp of Garlic Powder
- 1 Tsp of Onion Powder

Directions:

1. Spice up your regular backyard BBQ with an inviting rendition of an Italian classic. Check out this Caprese Grilled Chicken recipe for flavor that won't disappoint.
2. Preheat the grill to medium-high heat. Be sure grates are lightly oiled. Season the chicken breast with salt, pepper, oregano, dried basil, cayenne pepper, garlic powder and onion powder. Place chicken on the grill. On the stove, combine balsamic vinegar and butter. Place on high heat until boiling then reduce to low heat and simmer until reduced by half. Reduction should be thickened. Once chicken is nearly finished, top each breast with a slice of mozzarella. Cook for a few additional minutes until melted. Remove the chicken from the grill and top each breast with a tomato slice and basil. Drizzle to your liking with reduction. Serve immediately, enjoy!

Smoked Pimento Cheese Spread

Cooking Time: 2 To 4 Hrs

Ingredients:

- 1 Pound Extra-Sharp Cheddar Cheese (Block of Cheese)
- 8 Ounces Cream Cheese, Softened

- 1 Cup Sour Cream (Extra if making Spider Web Garnish)
- 1 Cup Mayonnaise
- 1/2 tsp Garlic Powder
- 1/2 tsp Ground Cayenne Pepper
- 1/2 tsp Onion Powder
- 1 Jalapeno Pepper, Diced
- 8 oz Jar Diced Pimentos, Drained
- Salt and Pepper to Taste

Directions:

1. Prepare grill for indirect smoking. Light between 4 to 6 briquettes or about a quarter chimney starter of lump charcoal.
2. Add fully ashed over charcoal to one side of the grill and place a handful of soaked wood chips on the coals.
3. Close the lid and close all the dampers almost all the way.
4. You want the temperature to be as low as possible,
5. Place the blocks of cheese on a wire rack.
6. Fill a drop pan with ice and place the rack on top of the pan filled with ice.
7. Place the pan and the rack with the cheese on the grill on the opposite side of the charcoal.
8. Add more wood chips when needed to maintain smoke.
9. Remove cheese from grill after 2 to 4 hours depending on desired level of smoke.
10. Grate cheese and add to large bowl.
11. Combine cheese with cream cheese, sour cream, mayonnaise, jalapeños, pimentos, and all spices. Mix well.
12. Transfer to serving bowl.
13. To make it spooky, place some sour cream in a plastic bag and cut off the tip of the bag. Use the bag and sour cream to create a spider web design on top of cheese spread.
14. Serve with chips, crackers, or veggies.

Grilled Eggs Benedict With Grilled Lemon Hollandaise

Cooking Time: 20 Min

Ingredients:

- 10 Eggs
- 4 English Muffins
- 8 Slices of Canadian Bacon
- 2 Lemons, Halved
- 1 Stick Unsalted Butter, Melted
- 1 Tbsp Dijon Mustard
- 1 Tbsp Salt

Directions:

1. From Aubrey:
2. "It's the week of Christmas and I couldn't be more thrilled to be spending my first 'warm' Christmas right here in my new home- the sunshine state. Usually the holidays are filled with blustery winds and snow, but this year, I'm thinking beach, and a grilled brunch. Who is with me!? Let's do a fun spin on everyone's favorite- Eggs Benedict. The star to the show is the lemon in the hollandaise sauce, so lets grill it. The best part about the grill?? Not having to clean up 7 different pans in one meal. This eggs benny is on your plate in less than 10. Plus- my hollandaise sauce is made in the blender, it's so easy! Let's do it! Happy Hollindaze! Ha!"
3. Preheat your Char-Griller Grill to high, and scrape those grates, we don't want any muffins sticking.
4. While our grill heats up, slice English muffins in half, and prepare the eggs for the hollandaise.

5. Separate 4 eggs, placing the yolks in a blender, and saving the whites for another day! (think omelet vibes).

6. Head out to the grill and grill your Canadian bacon, English muffins, and halved lemons, until crispy and golden brown. Pull from heat.

7. Cook remaining eggs to your liking, I love mine poached, but you can do sunny side up, or even scrambled.

8. In the blender with the yolks, squeeze the juice of 2 of the grilled lemon halves, and blend on high for 60 seconds, until light and fluffy. Add Dijon, salt, and pulse till combined. Then, while the motor is running slow, slowly drizzle in your melted butter until a thick and creamy hollandaise sauce has formed. It's really that easy!

9. Assemble the plates with English muffin, a slice of grilled bacon, an egg, and a dollop of your hollandaise. Garnish with fresh herbs and remaining grilled lemon pieces. Repeat until a Christmas nap appears, that's my gift to you! Enjoy!

Sweet N' Spicy Bbq Sauce

Cooking Time: 2 Min

Ingredients:

- 1 Cup Of Ketchup
- 3/4 Cup Brown Sugar
- 1/4 Cup Honey
- 1/8 Cup Apple Juice
- 1/4 Cup Apple Cider Vinegar
- 1/4 Cup Water
- 1 Tbsp Worcestershire Sauce
- 2 Tsp Of Yellow Mustard
- 1 Tsp Of Paprika
- 1/2 Tsp Of Crushed Red Pepper
- 1/2 Tsp Of Cayenne Pepper
- 1/2 Tsp Of Garlic Powder
- 1 Tsp of Sea Salt
- 1 Tsp Of Black Pepper

Directions:

1. Combine all the ingredients into a saucepan. Whisk them together until it's smooth and add to medium-high heat. Bring to a boil. Reduce the heat and allow to simmer for 2 minutes, continuing to stir occasionally. Let cool for about 10 minutes before storing in the refrigerator in an airtight container.

Caribbean Jerk Pork Pineapple Salsa

Cooking Time: 20 Min

Ingredients:

- Pork Tenderloin - 1 to 2 Pounds
- Jerk Seasoning - 2 Tablespoons
- Whole Pineapple - 1
- Olive Oil - 1 Teaspoon
- Charcoal
- Additional Pineapple, Chopped - 1 Cup
- Large Tomatoes, Chopped - 2
- White Onion, Finely Chopped - 1/2 Cup
- Jalapeno (seeds removed to preference), Finely Chopped - 1/2 Jalapeno
- Pineapple Juice - 2 Tablespoons

Directions:

1. Jerk Pork Directions:
2. Remove all excess fat and silver skin from the pork tenderloin. Use the olive oil as a slather on both sides of the pork tenderloin to help get the rub to stick. Carefully season both sides of the pork tenderloin with the jerk seasoning making sure it has a nice even coat.

3. Let the pork tenderloin rest and absorb the seasoning while you prep the pineapple. Split the pineapple vertically and use a knife and spoon to hollow one side of the pineapple out (this will be the presentation side.) Be sure to save the pineapple as it will be used later for the salsa.
4. Start prepping your fire and working on getting your grill up to 325 F. Once your grill has reached 325 F put the pork tenderloin on indirect heat. Once the pork tenderloin has reached around 150 F internal move it to direct heat and sear it until internal is 160 F. Pull the pork tenderloin and let rest for 10 minutes. Cut up into 1 ½ inch cubes and serve with pineapple salsa. Enjoy! *Tip* While your grill is hot put some pineapple on it to add an extra layer of flavor to your salsa.
5. Pineapple Salsa Directions:
6. In a bowl combine the pineapple, onion, jalapeno and pineapple juice. Let marinate for 3-5 minutes.
7. Add chopped tomatoes into the bowl with the other ingredients. Stir well.
8. Let the mixture marinate so the flavors can meld. Serve and enjoy! *Tip* If you let the pineapple salsa marinate for 1-3 hours the flavors will have time to meld together.

Garlic Bacon Green Beans

Cooking Time: 20 Min

Ingredients:

- 1 Pound Fresh Green Beans, Ends Trimmed
- 1/2 tsp Salt
- 1 Tbsp Olive Oil
- 1 Tbsp Butter
- 8 Garlic Cloves, Minced
- 6 Strips of Bacon, Cooked and Chopped

Directions:

1. Prepare charcoal grill for direct medium-high heat.
2. Fill a large pot more than halfway with water. Bring to boil.
3. Add green beans (water should cover all the beans), and salt. Cook for 5 minutes on medium heat then drain the beans.
4. Heat olive oil and butter in a large skillet over medium-high heat coals.
5. Add minced garlic, constantly stirring, for about 30 seconds.
6. Add cooked bacon and green beans. Saute on medium-high heat for about 1-2 minutes stirring to combine. Remove from heat.
7. Serve immediately and enjoy!
8. Optional topping: Toasted Sliced Almonds

Buttery Cinnamon Apples

Cooking Time: 30 Min

Ingredients:

- 8 Apples
- Cinnamon (To Taste)
- Sugar (To Taste)
- 2 Sticks Of Butter
- 1/4 Cup Of Brown Sugar

Directions:

1. First, you're going to want to peel your apples, at least I'm going to want to. You can leave the skins on if you want, I prefer them almost applesauce level of soft.
2. Whether you leave the skins on or off, you definitely want to remove the core. Only a complete lunatic would leave the core in the apple and try to eat it.
3. I used about 8 apples in my cook, and added two full sticks of quartered butter to them. No

need to premelt, your smoker is going to do that work.

4. Now you'll want to hit it with a generous helping of cinnamon and sugar. You really can do this to your taste, I'm going to go heavy, because, I mean, I'm not doing this for health and prosperity over here.

5. We are going to toss them in the smoker at 300 degrees for about a half an hour, and then we are going to pull them, and add about ¼ cup of brown sugar.

6. Toss it back in the smoker, mine took about another 30 minutes, and that's it. It's probably the easiest thing you'll ever cook.

Flavor Pro Smoked Eggs

Cooking Time: 1.5 Hrs

Ingredients:

- Dozen Large Eggs
- Char-Griller AP Seasoning
- Salt to Taste

Directions:

1. Prepare the Flavor Pro for indirect heat at 350°F. For best results, fill the far right zone of the Flavor Drawer with your favorite lump charcoal and a couple of small sized wood chunks. Ignite the far right burner to allow charcoal to light. Once fully lit, turn burner to off position and adjust your two smoke stacks to maintain temp at 350°F. Now you're ready for the eggs.
2. Place eggs directly on the grate but the opposite side, away from the heat. This will allow the eggs to "bake" on the grill.
3. Bake for 30 minutes then place the eggs in ice cold water to stop them from cooking any further. Over cooking the eggs can make them rubbery.
4. Once cooled, peel the shell off each of the eggs.
5. Note: This can sometimes be a bit difficult but I find that gently tapping and rolling them across a hard surface helps make this process a little easier. Your eggs may not peel clean every single time, and that's okay. They will still be just as delicious.
6. Next, set your Flavor Pro up for smoking. Add 6 pieces of charcoal to the far right side of the Flavor Drawer and light them using the far right gas burner. Add a few of your favorite wood chunks.
7. Note: Be sure not to let the pit temperature get above 185°F for smoking the eggs. 150°F is where I like to be for this recipe. For temperature adjustments, you can turn the far right burner to low or add more coals to get the temp to climb if it happens to dip. Make sure your wood chunks are always lit and are giving off smoke during the entire smoking process. For the smoke stacks, I kept the stack closest to the heat (right) closed and the far stack (left) 25% of the way open. Adjust as needed.
8. Season all sides of the eggs with the Char-Griller AP seasoning.
9. Place eggs back on the grill, directly on the grate. Again on the opposite side, away from the fire.
10. Smoke your eggs for 30-90 minutes.
11. Note: The longer they smoke, the more smoke flavor they will have. I find that 45 minutes of smoke is a great balance of flavor. You will notice your eggs will change color. The longer you smoke them the browner they get.
12. Once smoked, you can refrigerate to chill them if needed.
13. Serve and enjoy! I like to serve mine chilled, sliced in half, and salted!

Candied Bacon Recipe

Cooking Time: 35 Min

Ingredients:

- 9 Slices of Bacon
- Brown Sugar - 1/3 Cup
- Cinnamon - 1/4 tsp
- Black Pepper - 1/4 tsp

Directions:

1. Heat grill to 350 indirect heat. Combine brown sugar, cinnamon, and pepper in a small bowl. Dip each piece of bacon, front and back, in sugar mixture. Place bacon strips on a greased wire rack. Sprinkle remaining sugar over bacon. Place rack on the grill grates and cook bacon for 30-35 minutes until crispy. Remove from grill and allow to cool. Chop the bacon into small pieces. Place a small handful of bacon aside for topping. Make the bourbon glaze.

Grilled Arrachera Pita

Cooking Time: 15 Min

Ingredients:

- 1-2 Pounds of Arrachera Steak
- Favorite Marinade
- Pita
- Pita Toppings: Tomatoes, Cheese, Onions, Ranch Etc.

Directions:

1. Make your favorite marinade. James used a combination of Char-Griller Steak Rub, Pompeian Olive Oil, Blues Hog Raspberry Chipotle, McCormick Parsley Flakes & fresh garlic.
2. Place the marinade in a bowl with the arrachera. Set in the fridge for roughly three hours.
3. Fire up your Char-griller Grill and preheat to high heat.
4. Tip: Arrachera/skirt steak is thin and is best when cooked quickly.
5. Remove the arrachera from the the marinade and allow to get to room temperature.
6. Place the arrachera on the grill over the hot coals for roughly 5-6 mins per side.
7. Remove the arrachera from grill and allow to rest for five minutes. Then chop it up into small pieces.
8. Warm the Pitas on the grill for a few seconds on each side and remove.
9. Create the pita by adding the arrachera and then top it off with tomatoes, onions and then drizzle it with ranch.
10. Enjoy!

Smoked Chex Mix

Cooking Time: 1-1½ Hrs

Ingredients:

- 3 C. corn Chex cereal
- 3 C. rice Chex cereal
- 3 C. wheat Chex cereal
- 1 C. mixed nuts
- 1 C. mini pretzels
- 6 Tbsp. unsalted butter
- 2 Tbsp. Worcestershire sauce
- 1½ Tsp. seasoned salt
- ¾ Tsp. garlic powder
- ½ Tsp. onion powder
- 1 Tsp. cayenne pepper, optional

Directions:

1. Pre-heat grill to 250°F. Melt butter in a small pan and mix in Worcestershire sauce, seasoned salt, onion powder, garlic powder, and cayenne pepper, if using. 2. Place Chex cereal, mini

pretzels and mixed nuts in a large roasting pan. Add melted butter mixture and stir to evenly coat.
3. Place pan on the grill and smoke at 250°F for 1-1 ½ hours, and stir every 15-20 minutes. 4. Remove pan from grill and spread smoked Chex mix on paper towel-lined plate to cool.
2. Store in an airtight container or storage bag. Enjoy!

Flat Iron Pineapple Coconut Pancakes

Cooking Time: 15 Min

Ingredients:

- 1 1/2 Cup of All-Purpose Flour
- 2 Tsp of Baking Powder
- 1 Tsp of Baking Soda
- 1/4 Cup of Sugar
- 1/2 Tsp of Salt
- 2 Large Eggs
- 1/4 Cup of Butter (Melted)
- 1 Tsp of Butter or Cooking Spray for Griddle
- 1 Cup of Crushed Pineapple
- 1 Cup of Shredded Coconut (Ground Finely)
- 1/4 Cup of Coconut Milk

Directions:

1. In a large mixing bowl, prepare the batter by stirring together baking powder, baking soda, sugar, salt, eggs, butter, crushed pineapple, coconut, and coconut milk. Slowly add flour until you achieve a nice batter, not too runny and not too thick. Mix until it is smooth with no lumps.
2. Heat the Flat Iron over Medium-High Heat and spray with cooking spray or melt butter. Pour pancake batter onto griddle with amount depending on desired size of pancakes.
3. When lots of bubbles form on top, flip over and cook the other side until lightly browned.
4. Serve warm and drizzle with honey or maple syrup.

Brazilian Smoked N' Seared Picanha

Ingredients:

- Picanha (3-4 Pounds)
- 1 Whole Pineapple (Cut Into Squares Only Half Is Needed.)
- Brazilian Salt To Taste For The Picanha
- Habanero Sea Salt To Taste For The Pineapples
- Trompo King Meat Stacker Or Skewers
- Fogo Eucalyptus Lump Charcoal
- Char-Griller Grills Ceramic Akorn
- Char-Griller Grills Smokin' & Pizza Stones
- Char-Griller Grill Gloves

Directions:

1. Prepping Directions
2. Cut Pineapples into small squares. Only ½ of the pineapple will be needed. Rinse the Picanha using cold water and pat dry with a paper towel. Remove any loose fat from the top and bottom of the meat but don't remove off to much fat. The fat on Picanha tastes great and provides tremendous flavor to the meat during the cooking process. Slice the Picanha into two inch thick strips. Use Slice the meat diagonally going with grain. When the meat is sliced when it's done is when you slice against the grain. Apply even layer to taste of Brazilian Salt to all sides of the Picanha. Season all sides of the pineapples squares with Habanero Sea Salt to taste Using a Trompo King or Skewers, stack the Picanha curving the meat into a C shaped form and also stack the pineapples.
3. Smoking/Searing Directions

4. Ignite lump charcoal and preheat grill to 300°. Add the Char-Griller Grills Smokin' Stone & Pizza Stone for the smoking portion of the cook. Add the Trompo King or Skewers with the Picanha to the grill/smoker. Smoke the Picanha until internal temperature 125° is met, takes about 40 minutes. Remove the Trompo King or Skewers with the Picanha from the grill/smoker and set aside. Remove the Char-Griller Grills Smokin' Stone & Pizza Stone using a Char-Griller Grills Grill Glove and place under the grill/smoker. Time to sear the Picanha to internal temperature: 135° Add a bit more lump charcoal to the grill/smoker, insert the grill grates, open up the top and bottom vents to allow the grill/smoker to get hot: 420° and over. Place the Picanha onto to the grill/smoker grates for two minutes each side or until internal temperature 135° is reached. Remove the Picanha from the grill/smoker, add additional Brazilian salt to taste. Allow the meat to rest for 10-25 minutes before slicing. Slice the Picanha against the grain and enjoy

Grilled Romaine Salad With Creamy Jalapeno Ranch Dressing

Cooking Time: 20 Min

Ingredients:

- Bacon - 6 Strips
- Cherry Tomatoes - 10.5 Ounces
- Sweet Corn - 2 Ears
- Romaine Lettuce (halved lengthwise) - 3 Heads
- Olive Oil - For Greasing
- Crumbled Cotija Cheese - 1 Cup
- Hard Boiled Eggs (Halved) - 4
- Flaky Sea Salt and Ground Pepper
- Mayonnaise - 6 Tablespoons
- Milk - 6 Tablespoons
- Sour Cream - 1/4 Cup
- Dried Parsley - 1/4 Teaspoon
- Onion Powder - 1/4 Teaspoon
- Chopped Chives - 1 Tablespoon
- Garlic - 1 Clove
- Coarse Kosher Salt - 1/4 Teaspoon
- Ground Pepper - 1/4 Teaspoon
- Lime Juice - 2 Tablespoons
- Cilantro - 1/4 Cup
- Pickled Jalapeno - 4 Slices

Directions:

1. For the salad:
2. Cook the bacon: Place bacon strips in a cold large nonstick skillet. Turn the heat to medium and cook for 8-12 minutes, turning occasionally, until brown and crispy. Transfer to a large plate covered in paper towels and set aside to cool.
3. Preheat grill to medium-high heat (about 400°F-450°F) for direct-heat grilling.
4. For Gas Grilling: Simply light all the burners on low, close the lid and let the grill heat up for 5-10 minutes.
5. For Charcoal Grilling: Open the lid and the bottom/side vents, remove the grill grates and set aside. Fill a chimney starter with charcoal briquettes. Place one or two fire starter cubes or wadded-up newspaper onto the charcoal grates and place the chimney starter on top. Light the cubes or newspaper underneath the chimney and let the briquettes heat up for 15 minutes. When the briquettes are lightly covered with ash, use a pair of heat-resistant insulated gloves and carefully spread out the hot coals in an even layer. Carefully place the cooking grates back on, close

the lid, open the top vent and let the grill heat up for about 5-10 minutes.

6. Skewer the tomatoes: While the grill is heating up, thread the cherry tomatoes onto 4 large metal skewers. (If using wooden skewers, be sure to soak the skewers in water for 20 minutes beforehand so they don't burn on the grill.)

7. Prepare the remaining ingredients: Brush or spray the ears of corn, cherry tomatoes and the inside of the romaine lettuce halves with olive oil or cooking spray.

8. Grill the corn: Grill the ears of corn with the lid closed for 10-15 minutes, turning occasionally, until corn is caramelized and dark brown spots appear on the kernels. Transfer to a large plate or baking sheet and set aside.

9. Grill the tomatoes and lettuce: Grill the tomatoes and lettuce cut-side down with the lid open for about 3 minutes. Turn the tomatoes occasionally and remove when charred and blistered. Remove the lettuce when the cut-side is slightly charred. Be careful not to grill too much or the lettuce will wilt. Transfer to a large plate or baking sheet and set aside.

10. Cut the corn and crumble bacon: Cut the grilled corn off the cob and crumble the cooled bacon.

11. Serve: Place grilled lettuce cut-side up on a large serving platter and season with salt and pepper. Drizzle with creamy jalapeno ranch dressing and top with grilled corn kernels, grilled cherry tomatoes, crumbled bacon, cotija cheese and hard boiled eggs.

12. For the dressing:

13. Add all ingredients to a blender of food processor and blend until smooth.

14. (mayonnaise, milk, cup sour cream, dried parsley, onion powder, chopped chives, plus more for garnish, garlic, coarse kosher salt, ground black pepper, lime juice, cilantro, pickled jalapeños)

Grilled Breakfast Sandwiches With Blueberry Chicken Sausage

Cooking Time: 20 Min

Ingredients:

- Ground Chicken - 1 Lb
- Fresh Blueberries - 1/3 Cup
- Fresh Sage - 1 Tbsp, finely chopped
- Pure Maple Syrup - 2 Tbsp
- Butter - 1 Tbsp
- 6 Whole Wheat English Muffins
- 6 Eggs
- Shredded Cheddar Cheese - 1/2 Cup

Directions:

1. While the grill heats, combine ground chicken, fresh blueberries, sage, and half of the maple syrup. Form into 6 even patties and set aside. Mix remaining maple syrup with butter for maple butter.

2. Next, cut English muffins in half, and transfer eggs to a grill safe cooking pan. Top with salt, pepper, and cheese.

3. Once grill is hot, add sausage, English muffins, and eggs. Keep an eye on the English muffins- they only need about 1-2 minutes, just until they're toasted.

4. The sausage patties need 4 minutes per side, and the eggs will be done around the same time if you close the lid to help them steam.

5. Assemble the sandwiches- apply a layer of maple butter, and egg, and a sausage patty to each English muffin! Serve as is, or wrap in plastic

wrap for breakfast prep during the week. You can microwave them for 60 seconds and you have a hot breakfast ready to grab as you head out the door! Enjoy!

Smoked Sweet Potatoes

Cooking Time: 20 Min

Ingredients:

- (5) Sweet Potatoes or Yams
- Olive Oil
- Himalayan Pink Salt
- Thai Spice
- Sugar Free Maple Syrup
- Maple Cinnamon Seasoning
- Butter

Directions:

1. Start by venting the potatoes with a fork Brush EVOO on the potatoes, fully covering them Sprinkle with Himalayan pink salt Heat your grill to 300° Put the smoking stone in place Place your potatoes around the grill so they get indirect heat (This allows them to cook and absorb the smoke flavor without burning) Add a flavor chunk Flip the potatoes at the 1 hour mark Pull the potatoes when they are soft and have some give when you press in on them (Be careful as these will be extremely hot) Open the potatoes down the middle (Again, use caution as they will be hot) Use a fork to mix in Thai spice seasoning with the potato Add a dollop of butter and let it melt
2. Sugar Free Maple Cinnamon Butter
3. stick of butter, salted and soft SF Maple Syrup, 1/4 cup Maple Cinnamon Spice, 2 TBSP

Irish Nachos

Cooking Time: 15 Min

Ingredients:

- 3 Medium Size Russet Potatoes (Sliced 1/4 Thick)
- 1 Cup Shredded Cheese
- 4 Slices of Bacon
- 1 Green Onion (Sliced Thinly)
- Sour Cream
- Char-Griller Original Seasoning
- Sea Salt
- Oil

Directions:

1. Heat 2 middle burners on the flat iron to medium Add bacon slices and cook until crispy, flipping once during cooking. Slide bacon over to the side to stay warm while cooking the potatoes Increase heat to high and add a tablespoon or two of oil to griddle, over any remaining bacon grease and allow to heat up Add potato slices on top of oil and season with Char-Griller's seasoning and sprinkle evenly with salt Allow potatoes to crisp up, about 7-8 minutes and flip each slice over. Season again with Char-Griller's seasoning and salt and allow to get brown and crispy on the other side Remove bacon from griddle, crumble, and set aside Remove potatoes from griddle and add to an over safe plate. Add cheese and bacon and place plate directly back on the griddle. Cover with a melting dome or large metal bowl and allow cheese to melt Carefully remove plate with a pot holder when cheese is melted. Garnish with green onions and a spoonful of sour cream

Flat Iron Homestyle Hash Brown Patties

Cooking Time: 10 Min

Ingredients:

- 1 1/2 Lbs of Russet Potatoes
- 1 Tbsp of Fresh Chives (Minced)
- 1 Tbsp of Fresh Parsley (Minced)
- 1/2 Tsp of Salt
- 1/2 Tsp of Black Pepper
- 1/2 Tsp of Garlic Powder
- 1 Tbsp of Olive Oil or Canola Oil

Directions:

1. Wash, peel, and dry potatoes. Grate them into shreds then press with a paper towel to eliminate moisture.
2. Preheat Flat Iron to medium-high heat.
3. In a medium bowl, mix together grated potatoes, parsley, chives, salt, pepper and garlic powder in a bowl.
4. Drizzle oil on griddle.
5. Form potato mixture into patties and place on the griddle.
6. Cook each side for about 5 minutes or until crispy and golden brown.

RECIPE INDEX

www.ingramcontent.com/pod-product-compliance
Ingram Content Group UK Ltd.
Pitfield, Milton Keynes, MK11 3LW, UK
UKHW051132260726
13967UKWH00010B/3005